almond croissant

apricot Am bun

fennel Am bun

ALSO BY CHRISTINE MOORE
LITTLE FLOWER: RECIPES FROM THE CAFE

One of Food52's 16 Best Cookbooks of 2012—a Piglet finalist!

Winner, Best Nonfiction, Southern California Independent Booksellers Association Awards

"We're set to prepare and devour everything in it."
—*Wall Street Journal*

"This is a terrific book."
— Russ Parsons, *Los Angeles Times*

"A charming cookbook that needs to be left in the kitchen, not on the bookcase."
— Nancy Silverton, chef/owner of Mozza, founder of La Brea Bakery, and author of many cookbooks

"You can't always have Christine Moore around to explain her perfect blood orange tarts,
but *Little Flower* may be close enough."
— Jonathan Gold, Pulitzer Prize-winning food writer for the *Los Angeles Times*

ADVANCE PRAISE FOR
LITTLE FLOWER BAKING

"What a fabulous treat! I've always admired Christine's knack for making recipes that are both comforting and inspired. This is *the* book to use for updated baking essentials, full of secrets that are simple, uncomplicated, and delicious."

— Sherry Yard, owner/chef of the Helms Bakery
and author of *Desserts by the Yard* and *The Secrets of Baking*

"Reading these pages is like sitting with Christine for a cup of coffee. I can hear her voice in every hearty potato bacon biscuit, in how she tells us to make an earnest sauce out of sea salt caramels, and in the practical ways she suggests to swap one ingredient for the other when the season calls for it. Few bakers can translate their pastries into words with the richness that Christine and Cecilia have in this cookbook. This is the kind of book that finds a home on the kitchen counter, collecting stains from sticky fingers or splattering pots of fruit, with many of its pages marked and handwritten notes on the sidelines."

— Roxana Jullapat, baker, Friends + Family

"When you eat Christine Moore's food, you feel happy and well served by life."
— Jonathan Gold, Pulitzer Prize-winning food writer for the *Los Angeles Times*

"It's no surprise that Christine Moore's *Little Flower Baking* is just like her, straightforward and enormously appealing—always figuring out a way to teach or be of service, and ultimately luscious without being precious in any way. I want to bake my way through these recipes from the first to the last."

— Evan Kleiman, host of *Good Food* on KCRW/NPR

LITTLE FLOWER BAKING

Christine Moore

with Cecilia Leung • Photographs by Staci Valentine

PROSPECT
PARK·
BOOKS

CONTENTS

FOR THE LOVE OF BAKING

By Christine Moore

Blondies with spiced gumdrops (my favorite childhood pastry invention)... Rice Krispie treats with double marshmallow... rugelach made with scrap pie dough. The signs were all there.

"Do what you loved as a child." I'll never forget when someone said that to me when I was in my twenties, waiting tables.

Baking was something I loved. And when I was a kid, I used to write a menu for my mom before I brought in breakfast in bed. What kid does that? I'll tell you: one destined to serve. I wasn't a great brain in school; I actually never really liked school. I had wonderful friends and was good at sports, but I didn't follow the path that my friends did. The restaurant business turned out to be a safe place for a kid like me to land. It was a family of sorts. I've always felt very lucky to be in this community of hard-working people who feed and serve others and are nice to them. In other words, hospitality professionals.

Serving makes me feel good. It's who I am. Feeding people is a true honor. I tell my staff that we have more than 200 opportunities a day to make someone happy. That's a gift.

In my late twenties, after years in Los Angeles of waiting tables, managing restaurants, and catering, I finally decided to go to the back of the house and do what I loved as a child: bake. I took a few extension courses and was inspired by a teacher who had lived in France.

Then, when I was twenty-eight, a tragedy woke me up to the power of NOW. My dearest friend, Vonnie, died in a car accident. She was like a sister, and her stunning, unfathomable death both crushed me and made me realize how precious life is. How easy it was to die. It could happen. It did happen.

I was on a plane to Paris within a month. I knew no French, knew no one there, and had no plans other than a reservation for a hotel room for just three days, but I was ready to bite the apple of life. My ignorance really was bliss, and that year in Paris changed the course of my life. It made me rethink who I thought I was, and led me to realize who I really was and what I wanted. I owed all this to Vonnie.

I met a fantastic friend my first day there. He was working at Le Bioux, a wine shop across from my hotel, La Louisiane on rue de Seine in the 6th. After spending my first day walking the city, too petrified to speak to anyone, I went into the wine shop and said basically the only thing I knew how to say in French: "Je m'appelle Christine." The shopkeeper burst out laughing and said, in perfect English, "Do you always introduce yourself when you walk into a shop?" *Hooray*, I thought, *he's American!* Juan Sanchez and I have been lifelong friends since that moment.

Juan helped me get my *stage* at Gérard Mulot. He opened his home, cooked for me, and taught me how tremendous a man could be. I will be forever grateful to you, Juan, for how you guided me and watched over me.

Surviving in a foreign country is not as romantic as it seems in books and movies. I had a very limited amount of money saved, and kitchen work in Paris is tough. Working in those kitchens made me realize how incredibly easy we have it in the States. We'd go to work at 5 a.m., when it was dark out, and work until 7 p.m., when it was dark out again. Not seeing the sun for days plays tricks on your mind, especially this adopted daughter of California.

And yet I was so lucky to be able to work in Monsieur Mulot's kitchen. He was a formidable chef. The pastries, breads, and chocolates that he and his crew produced were, in my opinion, the best in the city. The smells of that kitchen will stay with me forever. On my most recent visit, I walked into his patisserie and tears welled up. It was twenty-five years ago, and it still feels like yesterday. Thank you, Monsieur Mulot.

I also had the great pleasure of working for a lovely chef at the Charcuterie de Seine. One day while chopping ham, I cut off the tip of my finger. I got woozy, but I didn't want to make a fuss, so I excused myself for a minute, bandaged it up, and got back to work. My finger bled for three days, and it hurt like crazy, but there was no crying in that kitchen.

Another day, the butcher delivered at least twenty pig's heads and two large buckets of blood. I looked up

from my work table and was stunned to see a large stainless steel table piled high with the heads: oozing, eyes open or shut, blood dripping on the floor. The chef came in, stuck his whole arm into a bucket of blood, seasoned it with white pepper, stirred and tasted it, and proceeded to begin splitting the pig's heads with an ax. I'm sure I held my breath, but I did not pass out. I prayed that he would stay and not leave me alone in the *cave* with all the pig's heads. But of course, that's exactly what he did. I refused to look up for fear that they'd start talking to me. I didn't look up until it was time to leave. Remembering that time, I can't stop thinking about how real the food in France was, because it wasn't wrapped in plastic and you knew where it came from. It taught me respect.

Living in Paris also made me fall in love with good butter: fragrant, salted, dense, and *so* flavorful. Many days I lived on nothing but a piece of fruit and a baguette with butter. I worked unpaid my whole time there, so I had to live off my small savings. I had no car, I wore the same jeans every day, and I had one chef's coat that I cleaned every night and hung on my radiator. These were the days before cell phones and internet, so I was stuck with my own thoughts and feelings, with my memories of home and of Vonnie, and with my dreams of the brilliant possibilities that lay ahead. All this gave me the guts to pop a postcard in the mail to my baking idol. More on that later.

When I returned to L.A. after a year, I went right to work, first for Larry Nicola and then for David Wynns at Les Deux Cafés. David was demanding and passionate, brilliant and beautiful, and we were inseparable. He challenged me, scolded me, required of me, gave to me, and introduced me to a whole new world: the farmers' market! We shopped the Sunday Hollywood market every week, long before it was a scene. We had almost no refrigeration and stored our produce in a warehouse next to the restaurant. Les Deux was a one-of-a-kind place

with one-of-a-kind people. The owner, Michele Lamy, was the most captivating person I'd ever met. She wore gauzy, dripping clothes and gold bangles, smelled of an amber perfume, and spoke in a smoky voice with a mysterious accent. I loved her. Her restaurant was *the* scene in the '90s, full of writers, actors, chefs, and other famous people, a whirlwind of drama and beauty and, I'm sure, many other things. (I walked into my pastry kitchen one morning to find a very famous singer passed out on the floor.) The servers were super-bitchy French girls, all of whom were beautiful and sassy.

Back to that postcard I sent from Paris: It was to Nancy Silverton. Ever since I'd decided to bake, I'd dreamed of working for her, but I never thought it would happen. And then one night, she came to dinner at Les Deux with Ruth Reichl. I was plating desserts that night, and David came by my station to make sure their desserts were perfect. I was so nervous. This was it. I was serving my idol, and she was with Ruth Reichl, the editor of *Gourmet*!

I didn't meet Nancy that night, but I fed her, and that was enough. It was David's night. He was the chef, and understanding your place in line is essential in a kitchen. I learned early on that you *never* step out of line in the kitchen. I did a TV segment one time, and when the director said "cut," the makeup crew came into the kitchen and started brushing my hair and touching up my makeup. It was the worst feeling ever, going against all my training. Brushing hair in the kitchen?! Yikes—you get fired for that!

The cream does rise to the top, but only when it's ready.

Eventually, I got to meet Nancy Silverton, and not only did she remember the postcard I'd sent her from Paris, but she told me she kept it pinned above her desk at Campanile. I couldn't believe it. I was lucky enough to work for her and her pastry chef, Kim Sklar, at Campanile. The pastry kitchen overlooked the dining room, and sometimes I'd look down on the candlelit tables and watch servers deliver the pastry plates and feel tremendous pride and joy.

In the fall of 1998, David Wynns asked me to go with him to Paris to cook dinner for Alice Waters. She was (according to David) being courted by the Louvre to open a restaurant, and he thought we should go and feed her. What a thrill! We served it on a rooftop in the Marais. David wrote the menu, and we shopped at the markets, and I made the dessert. Juan had his own wine shop by then, called La Dernière Goutte, and he chose the wine. Our dessert was something plum-based, with a wine sorbet, and I remember not loving it. Here was my moment to feed Alice Waters, and I didn't love my dessert! It was a big learning experience. I always ask my staff, "Do you love it?" Tapping into that passion is essential. If you don't love what you serve, others won't either.

I never met Alice that night, either. I saw her from across the room as she double-kissed David and presented him with a beautiful book that she'd signed. He was smitten, and we celebrated later that night with couscous and wine at Chez Omar. I remember that the wine tasted like pipe water. Nothing tasted good, and I was so tired.

When I got back to L.A., I found out that I was pregnant. I worked until a week before the delivery, and in May of 1999, my daughter Madeline was born.

I loved having Maddie, but I was not good at sitting still in our little house in Highland Park. I kept feeling like I should be peeling potatoes while I nursed. We kitchen people are used to constant movement. So I started to make candy. Lots of candy. I also made applesauce, caramel sauce, marshmallows—any sweet thing my heart desired. I made salty caramel and pecan caramels, hand-cut and not like the ones I grew up with, but like the ones I'd had in France: buttery and salty, firm and chewy. I'd give my prized bags and jars to friends and bring them as hostess gifts. I was in heaven. Making candy was always a luxury in the pastry kitchen—we were always too busy with production to play with sugar.

Back when I was still working at Campanile, I'd been inspired by Nancy's chocolate tart, a brilliant dessert with a layer of hard caramel and almonds beneath chocolate cream. I'd burned the sugar so many times when I was learning to make that tart that I became afraid to do it. (A caramel burn lasts forever! Hot, molten lava on your hand is enough to make you pass out.) But that experience made me a master at making dry caramel. Little did I know then that it would lead to an entire business.

As I made candy at home, I kept returning to the caramels. I brought a bag of them to my dear friend Teri

Gelber, who was the manager at La Brea Bakery. She and her husband Christopher tasted endless batches until they thought I had them just right. The salt had to be tender; the caramel, firm but not hard and definitely not soft. The wax paper had to be turned just so. When I felt it was right, I started selling them at farmers' markets.

Evan Kleiman interviewed me on KCRW about making artisan candy, because it was really the beginning of that movement. I did the interview with six-month-old Maddie sitting on my lap, chewing on a spatula. I never felt like a caramel expert. I was just obsessed with it, and salty ones hadn't been seen in L.A. before.

I made marshmallows because I could. Who had ever seen a square marshmallow flavored with vanilla bean? So those found an audience, too. They even earned me another interview with Evan Kleiman. Evan and my

supportive friends at KCRW put Little Flower on the map. For that I will be forever grateful.

After years of running a wholesale handmade candy business, I decided in 2007 to open a shop on a little strip of Colorado Boulevard on the western edge of Pasadena. Opening the bakery and getting back into the pastry kitchen was just what I needed. I had three kids by then—eight, six, and six months—and I needed a job. I did what I knew best. I baked and baked and baked. Once again, it changed the course of my life.

In the years since I opened Little Flower Cafe, I've had the pleasure of working with many bakers, some of whom are far more talented than I ever was or will be. For all of you who made Little Flower a stopping point along the way in your own magnificent careers, I am so thankful. For Cecilia Leung, the creative, brilliant, loyal pastry chef who has been by my side for years, I am particularly grateful.

Cecilia and I wrote this book, which my friend Staci Valentine has made so beautiful with her photographs, to share the recipes for all the delicious pastries we've made over the years.

Life is quite a journey, made even sweeter with pastries and candy.

MISE EN PLACE

Oh to be prepared! But keep it simple. Have a few basic pieces: some good bowls that you enjoy touching, some measuring cups and spoons that feel good in your hand. The one spatula and wooden spoon that you can't live without. The knife that is sharp, and the cutting board that is not too big to move around. These tools make cooking and baking doable and pleasurable. And keep your old mixers! They don't make them like that anymore. Instead of buying a new one, find a local machine shop to rebuild or fix that overheated KitchenAid.

Having to forage for all kinds of exotic ingredients can push your desire to bake to the back burner. The more you bake, the fresher your ingredients will be. Also, don't be afraid to try substitutes. One time, in the middle of a recipe, I had no buttermilk, so I added lemon juice to heavy cream. It turned out just fine.

Organize your ingredients, preheat your oven, prepare your basic doughs in advance, and, most importantly, have fun!

A FEW ESSENTIALS

The Egg Wash
It's quite common in recipes involving dough to finish with an egg wash, so be prepared to have an egg handy. Not only does an egg wash ensure even browning of the dough, but it also produces a beautiful sheen. To make the wash, simply whisk an egg! You can add a tablespoon of water if you like, or not. Use a pastry brush to apply.

Chilled Butter
Many recipes call for butter to be cut into 1/4-inch cubes and chilled. Because those little bits of butter will warm quickly, we cut the butter first and put it back in the fridge until we're ready to use it, so it stays cold.

Rotating Baking Dishes
In the majority of our recipes, you'll see that we advise rotating the baking dish halfway through the cooking process. Ovens are rarely flawlessly calibrated, and the hot spots can be uneven, so rotating helps ensure an even finish.

Freezing Until Firm
It's almost always a good idea to chill or even freeze dough before baking just about anything. It allows the dough to rest, and it helps the dry ingredients absorb the wet ones more slowly, which aids in marrying and developing the flavors. Also, freezing ensures that your baked goods hold their shape when they go into the oven.

   You should put all doughs in the freezer until firm. The amount of time varies depending on the size of what you're making—small cookies might firm up in just ten to thirty minutes, and larger doughs can take up to four hours. If you can plan ahead, overnight is best (good news for make-ahead folks!). You don't need to cover the dough for shorter-term freezing, but if it will be in there for more than three days, put it in a freezer bag to prevent freezer burn.

What Is Ribbon Stage?
When batter is at the ribbon stage, it incorporates air and ensures the suspension of the dissolved sugar in the eggs. This makes for a more tender crumb in the final cake. When you lift your whisk, batter will trail like a ribbon. The amount of time the ribbon holds determines the stability of the suspension. We recommend three to five seconds.

When to Sift Flour
After you measure it. Sifting aerates the flour and helps make the final result light and airy, with a delicate crumb.

What Is Blind Baking?
Baking a crust before you add the filling.

Special Equipment
We try to keep it simple in the kitchen, but you will need some gear to bake effectively. A good stand mixer is essential, of course, as are rubber spatulas, a pastry brush, and a few sizes of whisks, including a balloon whisk. For pans, it's good to have a couple of standard half-sheet baking pans, a 10-inch pie pan, a few 9-inch cake pans, an 8-inch cake pan, a half-sheet cake pan, a couple of 6-cup (large) muffin tins, a standard-size 12-muffin tin, and, if you want to make a tart, an 8 1/2-inch fluted tart pan with removable bottom. If you want to make the Golden Milk Latte, you'll need a centrifugal extraction juicer, unless you have a place where you can buy turmeric juice and ginger juice.

   Other staples include a metal bench scraper, a three-inch-round cutter, a candy thermometer, and either pie weights or dried beans, which also work to weigh down a pie crust. And lots and lots of parchment paper!

smoked
salt

INGREDIENTS

Specialty Ingredients

Most of these recipes call for ingredients you can find at any decent market, but from time to time you'll see some more unusual things, from amaranth flour to ginger syrup to pretzel salt. Cookbooks used to have detailed resource guides, but in this internet age, you can find everything online. If you don't live near a Whole Foods, Sprouts, or good gourmet or health-food store, Google will take you to such quality vendors as Bob's Red Mill, Sur la Table, and Penzeys Spices.

Butter

When I trained in Paris, I learned the value of quality butter. It really makes a difference, so try to get the good stuff. We recommend salted Échiré; Straus salted and Vermont Creamery salted butter are fantastic substitutes.

Oils

Grapeseed oil is the most neutral in flavor compared to olive oil, canola oil, vegetable oil, and corn oil and has a higher smoking point. On these two points alone, we prefer using grapeseed oil in our baking. It is also lighter in weight and viscosity. Runner-up for neutral oil is canola-olive blend. A good extra-virgin olive oil (that means first cold press) should taste like the land it came from: grassy, green, fruity, peppery, or bitter. In the Olive Oil Cake, the flavor of the oil shines front and center—do not replace olive oil with any other oil for that recipe. If you have a very special olive oil, best eaten straight, I wouldn't recommend using that in a cake either.

Salts

We are particular about salt at Little Flower. Each salt, especially Maldon, pretzel, or Fleur de Sel de Guérande (gray sea salt from the Guérande region of Brittany), has a different structure, flavor, and purpose. Sea salt is called specified in the majority of these recipes, but kosher salt also works beautifully. We emphatically say no to Morton's table salt, because it has a strong iodine flavor. Since table salt is more chemically processed, the small grain size results in a saltier flavor. We prefer Diamond Crystal kosher salt because it dissolves nicely. As for sea salt, look for a finer-grained one for general cooking purposes.

Maldon, due to its crystalline pyramid structure, provides more crunch and a flavor punch of salt before dissolving in the mouth. That is why it is used specifically on the Chocolate Sea Salt Caramel Cookies, Salted Chocolate Bouchons, and Gluten-Free Peanut Butter Cookies. A substitution of salt would compromise the integrity of the product. The salt on the Potato Bacon Herb Biscuits, however, can be substituted. The Guérande gray salt in the Caramel Corn was specifically chosen to mimic the soft, tender salt flavor of Little Flower's sea salt caramels, but that can be substituted with kosher salt.

For the pretzel rolls and dogs, we recommend using pretzel salt, because pretzels are known for their coarse salt, but if you can't find it, you can use kosher salt.

Vanilla Beans

At the bakeshop we soak dried vanilla beans in vanilla extract. Not only do the beans add extra flavor to and fortify the vanilla extract, but also it is easier to split a soaked vanilla bean pod than a dried one. To split a vanilla bean pod, take the tip of a paring knife and run it down the center of the pod from one end to the other. Split one end open and hold it down against a flat surface with thumb and index finger. Then take the blade of the paring knife and scrape along the split vanilla pod to extract all the seeds.

BRISÉE DOUGH

Makes 2 9-inch quiches or 12 5-inch tarts

4 ½ cups (540g) all-purpose flour
2 teaspoons sea salt
1½ cups (342g) unsalted butter, cut into ¼-inch cubes and chilled
⅓ cup (74g) ice water (ice cubes removed)

In the bowl of a stand mixer fitted with the paddle attachment, combine flour and salt on low speed. Gradually add butter on low speed. Continue to mix until pea-size lumps form, about 2 minutes. Gradually add ice water until dough comes together. Entire amount may not be necessary. Continue mixing for 30 more seconds. Dough should feel tacky and supple but not sticky.

Transfer dough onto a lightly floured surface. Place about ½ cup flour in a small bowl to use as bench flour. Dip the heel of your hand into the flour and flatten any butter chunks in the dough with your hand. Use the heel of your hand to push and smear the butter away from you. This process is called *fraisage*. It yields a flakier crust because the thin layers of butter create steam as the liquid evaporates, and flat, thin pockets form between layers. Work quickly to keep the dough and butter cold.

After *fraisage*, gather the dough into a ball and divide in half. Form each half into a disk and wrap with plastic. Chill in the refrigerator for at least 2 hours. This allows the glutens to relax and prevents the dough from shrinking when it's rolled. Brisée dough may be stored in the refrigerator for 3 days before it begins to oxidize and turn gray.

CREAM CHEESE DOUGH

Makes one 12" x 20" rectangle

2 cups (240g) all-purpose flour
1 tablespoon + 1½ teaspoons granulated sugar
¼ teaspoon sea salt
½ cup + 2 tablespoons (171g) unsalted butter, cut into ¼-inch cubes and chilled
½ cup + 2 tablespoons (171g) cream cheese, cut into 1-inch cubes

In the bowl of a stand mixer fitted with the paddle attachment, combine flour, sugar, and salt on low speed. Add cold butter and mix on low speed until pea-size lumps form. Add cream cheese and continue to mix on low speed until mixture is shaggy and begins to form a ball.

Transfer dough to a lightly floured surface. Knead a few times to incorporate any loose pieces. Divide dough evenly in half, wrap with plastic, and chill for at least 30 minutes before using.

CREAM BISCUITS

Makes 12 2-inch biscuits

2 1/4 cups (270g) all-purpose flour
2 1/4 cups + 2 tablespoons (285g) cake flour
2 tablespoons + 3/4 teaspoon baking powder
2 1/4 teaspoons sea salt
3/4 cup (150g) granulated sugar, divided
2 1/2 cups (600g) heavy whipping cream
1 egg, for wash

In the bowl of a stand mixer fitted with the paddle attachment, combine flour, cake flour, baking powder, salt, and 1/2 cup (100g) sugar on low speed. Add cream and mix on low speed until dough just comes together. Dough will be shaggy and a bit dry.

Transfer dough to a lightly floured surface. Gently pat into a 1-inch-thick rectangle. Do not overwork. Dough should feel tacky, but not sticky. Use a chef's knife to cut dough into 2-inch squares. Place biscuits onto parchment-lined sheet pan. Beat egg in a small bowl. Use a pastry brush to apply egg wash. Sprinkle biscuits liberally with 1/4 cup (50g) sugar. Freeze overnight or up to 2 weeks in an airtight container.

Preheat oven to 375°. Bake, rotating halfway through, until golden brown, about 24 minutes.

PÂTE À SUCRE

Makes one 8 1/2-inch round tart

3/4 cup + 1 tablespoon (100g) all-purpose flour, plus more for dusting
3/4 cup + 3 tablespoons (110g) cake flour
1/4 cup (50g) granulated sugar
2/3 cup (152g) unsalted butter, cut into 1/4-inch cubes and chilled
1 egg yolk, cold
1 tablespoon + 1 teaspoon heavy whipping cream, plus more if needed

In the bowl of a stand mixer fitted with the paddle attachment, combine all-purpose flour, cake flour, and sugar on low speed. Gradually add butter and mix on low speed until pea-size lumps form, about 2 minutes.

In a small bowl, whisk yolk and cream together. Add yolk mixture to dough and combine on lowest speed until just incorporated. If dough is on the drier side, add another 1 teaspoon cream.

Transfer dough to a lightly floured surface. Place about 1/4 cup flour in a small bowl to use as bench flour. Dip the heel of your hand into the flour and flatten any butter chunks in the dough with your hand. Use the heel of your hand to push and smear the butter away from you. This process is called *fraisage*. It yields a flakier crust because the thin layers of butter create steam as the liquid evaporates and flat, thin pockets form between layers. Work quickly to keep the dough and butter cold.

Gather the dough, using a bench scraper to help scrape dough off surface. Form into a disk and wrap with plastic. Chill in the refrigerator for at least 2 hours. This allows the glutens to relax. Dough can be stored in the refrigerator up to 3 days before it begins to oxidize and turn gray.

Sandwich chilled dough between two lightly floured pieces of parchment paper. Roll dough into a 10-inch circle. Press into an 8 1/2-inch round tart tin. Press along edge of tart shell into corners of tart tin with your thumbs to prevent any air bubbles from forming between tin and dough. Freeze until firm, at least 1 hour.

Preheat oven to 350°. Lightly coat a round piece of parchment paper with nonstick spray and top dough shell with paper and pie weights. Bake until blond, about 20 minutes. Remove parchment paper and pie weights. Continue baking until golden and opaque, about 10 more minutes. Cool before filling.

TEFF PÂTE À SUCRE

Teff is an ancient grain that's small and mighty, packed with flavor and devoid of gluten.
Gluten-free

Makes one 8 ½–inch round tart

½ cup + 1 ½ tablespoons (82g) sweet rice flour, such as Koda Farms mochiko
½ cup + 1 ½ tablespoons (70g) buckwheat flour
⅓ cup (50g) potato starch
⅓ cup (45g) teff flour
¼ cup (50g) granulated sugar
⅔ cup (152g) unsalted butter, cut into ¼-inch cubes and chilled
1 egg yolk, cold
1 tablespoon + 1 teaspoon heavy whipping cream, plus more if needed

In the bowl of a stand mixer fitted with the paddle attachment, combine rice flour, buckwheat flour, potato starch, teff flour, and sugar on low speed. Gradually add butter and mix on low speed until pea-size lumps form, about 2 minutes.

In a small bowl, whisk yolk and cream together. Add yolk mixture to dough and combine on lowest speed until just incorporated. If dough is on the drier side, add another 1 teaspoon cream.

Transfer dough to a work surface and gather it, using a bench scraper to help scrape dough off surface. Form into a disk and wrap with plastic. Chill in the refrigerator for at least 1 hour. Dough can be stored in the refrigerator up to 3 days before it begins to oxidize and turn gray.

Sandwich chilled dough between two sheets of parchment paper and roll it into a 10-inch circle. Press into an 8 ½-inch-round tart pan. Press along edge of tart shell into corners of pan with your thumbs to prevent any air bubbles from forming between tin and dough. Freeze until firm, at least 1 hour.

QUICK PUFF PASTRY

Makes 2 14″ x 16″ sheets

4 cups (480g) all-purpose flour
1½ teaspoons sea salt
3¼ cups (741g) unsalted butter, cut into ¼-inch cubes and chilled
1 cup (222g) ice water, ice cubes removed

In the bowl of a stand mixer fitted with the paddle attachment, combine flour and salt on low speed. Gradually add butter until pea-size lumps form, about 2 minutes. Gradually add ice water on low speed until dough comes together. Entire amount may not be necessary. Continue mixing for 30 seconds.

Shape dough into a flat rectangle. Wrap in plastic wrap and chill for at least 1 hour in the refrigerator.

Lightly flour work surface and roll chilled dough into a 16″ x 28″ rectangle that is ¼ inch thick. Fold the dough into thirds, as if folding a letter. The turned dough should measure about 9″ x 16″. This is the first turn. Place on a parchment-lined sheet pan and wrap with plastic. Chill dough in the refrigerator for 15 minutes.

For the second turn, position the turned dough so that the seam side is facing you. Roll chilled dough into a 16″ x 28″ rectangle that is ¼ inch thick. Fold into thirds as described above and chill another 15 minutes. This is the second turn. Repeat two more times, for a total of four turns. Chill after each turn.

After the last turn is complete, roll out the chilled dough into a 16″ x 28″ rectangle that is ¼ inch thick. Trim edges and cut the dough in half, to yield 2 14″ x 16″ rectangles. Layer the puff pastry sheets, separated by a piece of parchment paper, on a parchment-lined sheet pan.

Wrap tightly in plastic wrap and freeze for up to 1 week.

BRIOCHE

Brioche is a rich, pillowy bread delicious on its own. At the café we use this dough as the base to our Apricot Morning Buns, Sticky Buns, Fennel Morning Buns, Hot Cross Buns, and Brioche Ring.

Makes 1 Pullman loaf

1 cup (235g) whole milk, room temperature

1 tablespoon + 1/4 teaspoon active dry yeast

5 1/4 cups (630g) bread flour, divided

1/2 cup + 1 tablespoon (113g) granulated sugar

1 tablespoon + 1/2 teaspoon kosher salt

6 large eggs, room temperature

3/4 cup (171g) unsalted butter, softened

1 egg, for wash

Combine milk and yeast in the bowl of a stand mixer. Whisk milk and yeast together by hand until yeast dissolves. Add 1 cup (120g) bread flour and sugar and continue to whisk by hand until ingredients resemble a thick slurry. This is the sponge.

Spread 4 1/4 cups (510g) bread flour evenly on top of the sponge, then place the salt on top. Do not let the salt touch the sponge, or it will kill the yeast. Cover with plastic wrap and set in a warm place to rise until sponge bubbles around edges and flour splits and cracks, 30 to 45 minutes.

Return bowl to a stand mixer fitted with the dough hook attachment. Add 6 eggs to sponge mixture and mix on lowest speed until combined, 3 to 5 minutes. Add butter in three additions, mixing on low speed after each addition until just combined. Scrape bowl well with a rubber spatula or plastic bowl scraper to incorporate all ingredients. Mix on lowest speed for 20 to 30 minutes. Dough will eventually make a slapping sound in the mixing bowl. You may need to hold on to the mixer to steady it.

Dough will look shiny and smooth and pull away from the mixing bowl, gathering around the dough hook. Check the gluten formation by using the windowpane test: pinch off a 1/2-inch ball of dough and stretch it out. It should be strong enough to stretch out into a thin, transparent sheet. Transfer dough into a large bowl lightly coated in oil or nonstick spray. Cover with plastic wrap and leave to rise until doubled in volume, about 2 hours.

Remove plastic wrap and punch dough down by taking the edge of one side of the dough and pulling it to the center. Repeat with the other three sides, so the seams are all in the center. Dough should be shiny and smooth. Rotate the dough so the seams are at the bottom of the bowl.

Cover with plastic wrap and let rise in the refrigerator until doubled in volume, about 4 hours. For the best flavor development, let it rise longer, 8 hours to overnight.

Remove dough from the refrigerator. Lightly coat a Pullman loaf pan with nonstick spray. Transfer dough to a lightly floured surface and roll it back and forth by hand to shape into a log. Place dough into prepared pan and set aside to proof until it has risen and is room temperature, about 2 hours.

Preheat oven to 375°. In a small bowl, beat egg. Use pastry brush to coat top of loaf with egg wash.

Place loaf pan on a sheet pan and bake 30 minutes. Rotate and continue baking until top of loaf is brown and internal temperature reads 200°, about 30 more minutes. Cool in pan and then unmold.

Variation: Bacon

Substitute bacon fat or rendered pork fat for the butter. Add 1/4 cup chopped, cooked bacon to dough after the first rise, as you fold over the edges.

PERFECT WHITE CAKE

Tender and moist, this is the ideal birthday or wedding cake.

Makes one 9-inch, 4-layer cake

2 cups (456g) unsalted butter, softened
3 1/2 cups (700g) granulated sugar, divided
8 large eggs, separated
4 teaspoons vanilla extract
4 3/4 cups + 1 tablespoon (580g) cake flour
1 tablespoon baking powder
3/4 teaspoon sea salt
2 cups (470g) whole milk

Preheat oven to 350°. Line 4 9-inch-round, 2-inch-tall cake pans with parchment and lightly coat with nonstick spray.

In the bowl of a stand mixer fitted with the paddle attachment, cream butter and 1 3/4 cups (350g) sugar on medium speed until pale and fluffy. Use a rubber spatula to scrape bowl well. Add egg yolks 2 at a time, mixing on medium-low speed until combined. Scrape bowl well. Add vanilla extract.

Sift cake flour, baking powder, and salt into a large bowl. Alternate adding dry ingredients and milk in 3 additions on low speed, starting and ending with dry ingredients. Scrape bowl well. Transfer batter to a large bowl and set aside.

In the dry, clean bowl of a stand mixer fitted with the whisk attachment, whisk egg whites on medium speed until frothy. Gradually add 1 3/4 cups (350g) sugar. Increase speed to high and whisk until mixture becomes a medium-stiff meringue. Test by dipping a spoon into the meringue—if it forms a glossy peak the shape of a bird's beak, it's ready.

Gently fold 1/2 cup meringue into batter with a rubber spatula to loosen. Continue to fold in remaining meringue with a balloon whisk: cut into the center of batter, then drag whisk toward you and up the side of the bowl. Rotate bowl a quarter turn each time meringue is folded into the batter. Continue to fold meringue in this manner until it is just combined and batter is airy and fluffy. Divide batter evenly between the 4 cake pans.

Bake, rotating halfway, until golden brown and a toothpick comes out clean, about 30 minutes. The cake should pull a little from the sides of the pan. Cool completely before unmolding.

Variation: Matcha
Substitute 3 tablespoons matcha powder for 3 tablespoons of the cake flour.

Tip: A balloon whisk helps maintain the air in a medium-stiff meringue when folding it into the batter. This will yield a delicate, tender cake crumb.

BASIC LAYER CAKE ASSEMBLY

½ cup (111g) water
½ cup (100g) granulated sugar
4 cake layers, any variety
1 quart Buttercream Frosting (*see page 33*), whipped, softened

Place water and sugar in a small saucepan to make a simple syrup. Bring to a boil and continue to simmer until sugar has dissolved. Let cool before using.

Place one cake layer on cake turntable. Use a serrated knife to go around the top edge of the cake layer to score it before leveling off the domed cake top, so you get a flat, even cake layer. Once scored and the height is the same around the cake, use the serrated knife in a sawing motion, going back and forth slowly to remove the cake dome (cake scraps make an excellent trifle!). Repeat for all four layers.

Place first layer of cake on turntable. Use a pastry brush to moisten the top of the layer with syrup evenly.

Spread ³/4 cup buttercream on top of cake with a small offset spatula. Make sure to spread all the way to the

edges of cake (but not on the sides). Place next cake layer on top, gently pressing down to make sure cake is even and secure. Repeat with each layer. Spread 1 cup buttercream on outside of cake, working the small offset spatula back and forth to cover entire exterior of the layered cake. Crumbs may fall off, but that's okay, the buttercream will act as a glue to adhere crumbs to the cake. Clean up and smooth the surface by keeping the offset spatula flat on top while spinning the cake turntable. For the sides, hold the offset spatula upright and turn cake turntable to smooth buttercream. This is the crumb coat. Chill in refrigerator 30 minutes.

Remove chilled layer cake. Spread 3/4 cup buttercream on top and sides of cake. Use small offset spatula to apply final coat of frosting. Decorate as desired.

Variation: Filled Cake

The cake's middle layers may be filled with custards, jams, fruit, or whatever you like. Place buttercream in a pastry bag fitted with a plain round tip and pipe a lip around the outside edge of the cake layer you wish to top with a filling, then add the filling inside the lip in an even layer.

CRISP TOPPING

Makes 1 quart

1 1/2 cups (180g) all-purpose flour
3/4 cup (150g) granulated sugar
3/4 cup (160g) golden brown sugar, packed
1/2 teaspoon sea salt
1 cup (228g) unsalted butter, cut into 1/4-inch cubes and chilled

In the bowl of a stand mixer fitted with the paddle attachment, combine flour, sugar, brown sugar, and salt on low speed for 1 minute. Gradually add butter and mix on low speed until pea-size lumps form, 3 to 5 minutes. Do not overmix; mixture should resemble wet sand. To test, take a handful of topping: It should hold together for 5 to 10 seconds before crumbling apart. Crisp Topping can be used right away or stored in an airtight container in the refrigerator for up to 2 weeks.

BROWN BUTTER

To make brown butter, place butter in a medium or large saucepan over medium-high heat. Heat butter until it foams and milk solids fall to bottom of pot. Use a rubber spatula to scrape the bottom so that milk solids brown evenly without burning. Let butter foam a second time. Butter should have a nutty aroma. Remove from heat and cool.

ALMOND CREAM

Makes about 1 1/2 cups

1/2 cup (114g) unsalted butter, softened
1/2 cup (100g) granulated sugar
1 cup (114g) finely ground sliced almonds
1 large egg, room temperature
1/8 teaspoon sea salt

In the bowl of a stand mixer fitted with the paddle attachment, cream butter and sugar on medium-low speed until mixture is pale and fluffy, 2 to 3 minutes.

Add ground almonds and continue to mix for 2 minutes. Scrape bowl well with a rubber spatula to prevent lumps. Add egg and mix until incorporated. Scrape bowl well. Add salt and continue to mix on medium speed until almond cream is fluffy and aerated, about 5 minutes. Store in an airtight container and refrigerate until ready to use. If aerated properly, almond cream should be spreadable when chilled.

BUTTERCREAM FROSTING

Makes 1 quart

1 cup (228g) unsalted butter, softened
3 ⅓ cups (417g) powdered sugar
1½ teaspoons vanilla extract
1 teaspoon sea salt
1½ teaspoons heavy whipping cream
1½ teaspoons whole milk

In the bowl of a stand mixer fitted with the paddle attachment, cream butter on medium speed until fluffy, about 2 minutes. Add powdered sugar in 3 additions on low speed. Scrape bowl well with rubber spatula after each addition. Add vanilla extract and salt and mix until incorporated. Scrape bowl well. Add cream and milk and mix on low speed until well incorporated. Scrape bowl well. Increase speed to medium-high and cream for 2 minutes. Transfer into a smell-free container. Use immediately or store covered in refrigerator up to 2 weeks.

Variations

Chocolate: Add 4 ounces melted bittersweet chocolate after powdered sugar is fully incorporated.
Brown Butter: Replace butter with an equal amount of brown butter (*see page 32*). Add an additional tablespoon of milk.
Coconut: Replace cream and milk with an equal amount of coconut milk.
Black Sesame: Add 1 tablespoon black sesame seeds, toasted and finely ground, and an additional ¼ teaspoon sea salt.

SEA SALT CARAMEL SAUCE

Makes 2 cups

½ pound (1 cup, or 228g) sea salt caramels
1 cup (240g) heavy whipping cream

Place caramels and cream in a medium saucepan over medium-low heat. Stir occasionally with a rubber spatula until caramels melt and sauce begins to simmer and come together. Cool and transfer to a container. Store sauce in the refrigerator for up to 2 weeks. Let sauce cool to room temperature before using.

MORE BASIC RECIPES

Throughout the book you'll find short, easy side recipes for glazes, frostings, icings, compotes, and such. These can work with many other dishes, or even on their own. Experiment and try some mixing and matching! Here's where to find them:

peach ricotta

Honey lavender

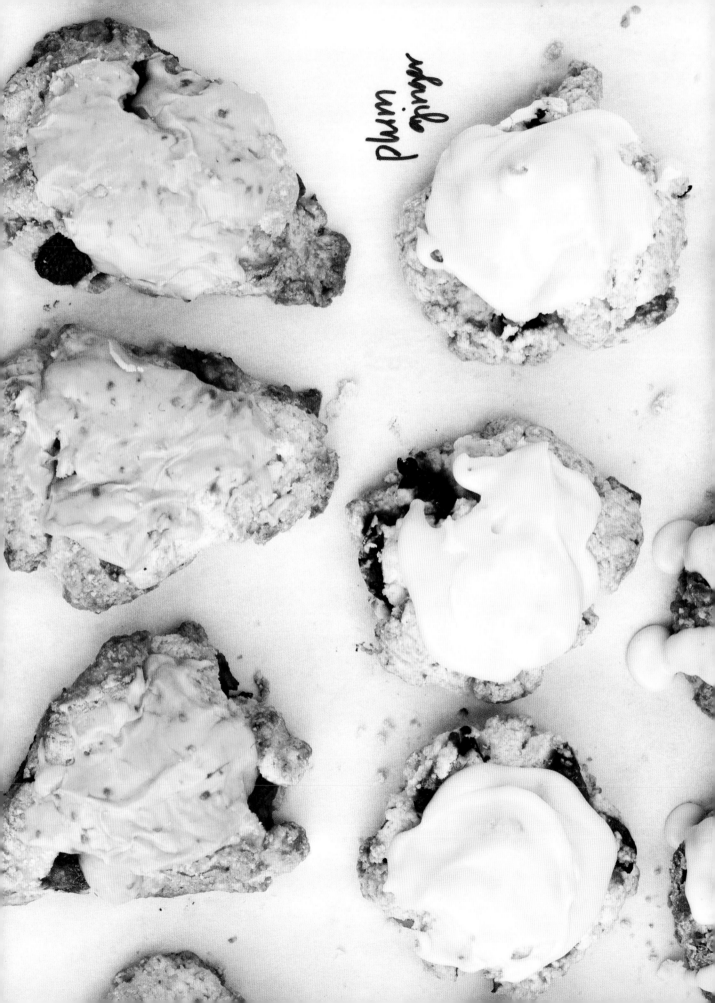

PASTRIES

When I lived in Paris, I would walk to work at 4:45 a.m. to get to the kitchen door by 5 a.m. The streets smelled like cigarettes and wine from all the late-night revelers. Sometimes those revelers were just stumbling home. Every block or so, I'd pass the back door of a boulangerie, whose empty flour sacks were tossed in the street. The aroma of baguettes and morning pastries was enough to make my head spin.

The few hours before daybreak, when you're baking the daily bread or pastry to help so many start their day, are some of the most beautiful moments—and meditations—a baker can experience. To open the doors of your shop and present your very best almond croissants, morning buns, and fresh muffins is an act of love. To feed people as they start their day is an honor.

These beautiful pastries start our days at Little Flower.

ALMOND CROISSANTS

I will never forget my first almond croissant, which I had while traveling around Europe as a teenager: fragrant French butter, crunchy toasted almonds, and a cream that pooled and candied into crispy, crunchy edges. These twice-baked treats are made with day-old croissants, a classic French way of using leftover bread.

Makes 12

½ cup (114g) unsalted butter, softened
½ cup (100g) granulated sugar
1 cup (114g) finely ground sliced almonds
1 large egg, room temperature
⅛ teaspoon sea salt
12 day-old butter croissants, halved lengthwise
1 cup (86g) sliced almonds
½ cup (63g) powdered sugar, for dusting

Preheat oven to 375°. Line two half-sheet pans with parchment paper. In the bowl of a stand mixer fitted with the paddle attachment, cream butter and sugar on medium-low speed until mixture is pale and fluffy, 2 to 3 minutes. Scrape bowl well with a rubber spatula to prevent any butter-sugar lumps. Add ground almonds and continue to mix on medium speed for 2 more minutes.

Add egg and mix on medium speed until fully incorporated. Scrape bowl well. Add salt and continue to mix on medium speed until almond cream is fluffy and aerated, about 5 minutes. Refrigerate in an airtight container until ready to use. If properly aerated, almond cream should be spreadable straight out of the refrigerator.

Press down on butter croissants to flatten them. Open a halved croissant and liberally spread 1 tablespoon almond cream on cut side of one half, coating entirely. Close the croissant and press to flatten. Spread 1 tablespoon almond cream on top of croissant, coating entirely. Repeat with remaining croissants. Place six almond croissants on each half-sheet pan. Sprinkle sliced almonds on each assembled croissant. Refrigerate or freeze until ready to bake. Almond croissants will keep, frozen, up to 2 weeks.

Bake, rotating pans halfway through, until golden brown, about 30 minutes. The almond cream will ooze out of the croissants and caramelize into crunchy bits (the best part!). Let cool for 10 minutes. Dust with powdered sugar and serve.

FENNEL MORNING BUNS

I love the flavor of licorice. These fennel-seeded buns are perfect for wintry mornings.

Makes 6

½ recipe (about 775g) Brioche dough *(see page 28)*
All-purpose flour, for dusting
2 tablespoons dark brown sugar
1 teaspoon fennel seeds, toasted and ground
1 teaspoon star anise, toasted and ground
½ teaspoon coriander, toasted and ground
¼ teaspoon sea salt
¼ cup (57g) butter, softened, to coat pan
¼ cup (50g) granulated sugar, to coat pan

Fennel Sugar

1 teaspoon fennel seeds, toasted and ground
½ teaspoon star anise, toasted and ground
¼ cup (50g) granulated sugar

Allow brioche dough to come to room temperature and line work surface with a sheet of parchment paper. Lightly flour parchment paper and transfer dough to parchment. Lightly flour dough and roll into a 9" x 12" rectangle that is ¼ inch thick. Arrange the rectangle in the landscape format, so the 12" side is in front of you.

Combine brown sugar, fennel, star anise, coriander, and salt in a small bowl. Spread sugar mixture evenly over dough. Starting from the short side, begin tucking and rolling the edge of the dough over the sugar, keeping it snug. It's important to roll the dough tightly, so the foundation is strong and it won't unravel later when the dough is cut. Continue to roll the dough similar to a jelly roll. Lift the parchment paper to help roll the dough up. Press on the seam to make sure it sticks. Wrap parchment around the rolled dough and freeze until firm, at least 1 hour.

Preheat oven to 375°. Use a pastry brush to lightly coat a 6-cup muffin tin with butter. Place 2 teaspoons sugar into each mold and coat evenly.

Remove dough log from freezer. Use a chef's knife to slice dough log into 6 2-inch buns and place in molds with swirl side up. Cover muffin tin loosely with plastic wrap. Set aside to proof in warm place until doubled in size, about 1 hour.

Bake until golden brown, about 36 minutes, rotating halfway through.

While buns bake, prepare Fennel Sugar: Combine fennel, star anise, and sugar in a medium bowl and set aside. Cool buns for 5 minutes before unmolding. Coat in fennel sugar and serve.

APRICOT MORNING BUNS

Just say "morning bun" and you feel like a gentle morning is waiting for you. Add apricot jam and these buns will be even more delicious.

Makes 6

½ recipe (about 775g) Brioche dough (*see page 28*)
All-purpose flour, for dusting
¼ cup (85g) apricot jam
3 tablespoons (43g) unsalted butter, softened
½ cup (100g) granulated sugar, divided

Allow brioche dough to come to room temperature and line work surface with a sheet of parchment paper. Lightly flour parchment paper and transfer dough to parchment. Lightly flour dough and roll into a 9" x 12" rectangle that is ¼ inch thick. Arrange the rectangle in the landscape format, so the 12" side is in front of you. With a small offset spatula, spread apricot jam evenly over dough.

Starting from the short side, begin tucking and rolling the edge of the dough over the sugar, keeping it snug. It's important to roll the dough tightly, so the foundation is strong and it won't unravel later when the dough is cut. Continue to roll the dough similar to a jelly roll. Lift the parchment paper to help roll the dough up. Press on the seam to make sure it sticks. Wrap parchment around the rolled dough and freeze until firm, at least 1 hour.

Preheat oven to 375°. Use a pastry brush to coat a 6-cup muffin tin with softened butter. Sprinkle 2 teaspoons sugar in each cup. Hold the tin upright at a slight angle and turn it clockwise to shake the sugar so that each compartment is coated with sugar.

Remove morning bun log from freezer and slice into 6 equal portions, about 2 inches thick. Place each bun in sugar-lined muffin cup, cut side up. Leave dough to proof in warm place until it is soft and pillowy, rising above rim of molds, about 1 hour.

Bake until golden brown, about 36 minutes, rotating halfway through.

Cool for 10 minutes before unmolding. Use a small offset spatula to loosen buns. If caramel is too cool to unmold properly, return tin to oven for 5 minutes and unmold. Toss in remaining ¼ cup sugar to coat. Serve warm.

AMARANTH MILLET MUFFINS

Cecilia experiments all the time with alternative flours that help with gluten intolerance and other digestive issues. Our customers love her for always having a treat for them in our dessert case. This muffin is hearty, beautiful, and gluten-free. If plums aren't in season, substitute any fruit you love!

Gluten-free

Makes 6

1/2 cup + 2 tablespoons (90g) brown rice flour

1/2 cup + 2 tablespoons (90g) teff flour

1/2 cup + 2 tablespoons (90g) amaranth flour

1/4 cup + 2 tablespoons (50g) potato starch

1 teaspoon baking powder

1/2 teaspoon baking soda

1/2 teaspoon sea salt

2 1/2 tablespoons (30g) whole millet

2 1/2 tablespoons (30g) whole amaranth

2 tablespoons chia seeds

1/2 cup (111g) water, boiling

1 cup (225g) soy milk

1 tablespoon apple cider vinegar

1/2 cup + 1 tablespoon (114g) coconut oil, melted

1/4 cup + 2 tablespoons (105g) brown rice syrup

4 plums, pitted, sliced 1/4 inch thick

Preheat oven to 375°. Lightly coat a 6-cup muffin tin with nonstick spray.

In a large mixing bowl, whisk together brown rice flour, teff flour, amaranth flour, potato starch, baking powder, baking soda, salt, whole millet, and whole amaranth. Set aside.

Place chia seeds in a small mixing bowl. Add boiling water and mix well. Set aside for 5 minutes, allowing chia seeds to absorb all the water. The chia seeds will plump up and become gelatinous.

In another small bowl, whisk together soy milk and apple cider vinegar. Set aside for 5 minutes, allowing the soy milk to curdle and create a nondairy buttermilk.

Add chia seeds, soy buttermilk, coconut oil, and brown rice syrup to flour mixture. Whisk until flours completely absorb wet ingredients. Divide batter evenly among muffin cups, filling each cup 2/3 full. Top each muffin with 3 plum slices.

Place on middle rack and bake 20 minutes. Rotate muffin pan and continue baking until juice from plum slices bubbles and becomes jammy and a toothpick comes out clean, about 15 more minutes. Let cool completely before unmolding.

PUMPKIN STREUSEL MUFFINS

Every fall, seeing pumpkins for sale and trees changing color reminds me to get this recipe out. The pepita streusel adds a wonderful crunch.

Makes 6

1 ¾ cups (210g) all-purpose flour
1 teaspoon baking soda
1 teaspoon sea salt
½ teaspoon ground nutmeg
½ teaspoon ground allspice
½ teaspoon pumpkin pie spice
½ teaspoon ground cinnamon
¼ teaspoon ground cloves
2 large eggs, beaten
1 ½ cups (300g) granulated sugar
½ cup (100g) grapeseed oil
1 cup (270g) pumpkin purée (or canned pumpkin)
½ cup (111g) water
¼ cup (55g) pepitas, for garnish
½ cup + 1 tablespoon Crisp Topping (see page 32)

Preheat oven to 375°. Line a 6-cup muffin tin with muffin liners.

Sift flour, baking soda, salt, nutmeg, allspice, pumpkin pie spice, cinnamon, and cloves into a large bowl and set aside.

In the bowl of a stand mixer fitted with the whisk attachment, mix eggs and sugar on low speed until combined, about 3 minutes. Scrape bowl well to prevent sugar from settling to bottom. Drizzle in oil and whisk on medium speed until combined, about 30 seconds. Add pumpkin purée and mix on medium speed for 20 seconds.

Add sifted dry ingredients and water alternately in 5 additions, starting and ending with dry ingredients. Mix on low speed for 5 to 10 seconds after each addition, until just incorporated. Do not overmix. Some dry bits are okay. Remove bowl from stand mixer. Scrape bowl well and fold in any dry bits using a rubber spatula.

Fill each muffin mold ⅔ full. Top each muffin with a sprinkle of pepitas and 1 ½ tablespoons crisp topping. Bake 15 minutes, rotate muffin tin, and continue baking until a toothpick comes out clean, about 12 more minutes.

ORANGE POPPYSEED MUFFINS

A classic combination.

Makes 6

2 cups (240g) all-purpose flour
½ cup (100g) granulated sugar
¼ cup (53g) golden brown sugar, packed
1 teaspoon baking powder
1 teaspoon baking soda
¼ teaspoon sea salt
½ cup (72g) poppyseeds
3 large eggs, room temperature
½ cup (120g) sour cream
1 tablespoon vanilla extract
½ cup (114g) unsalted butter, melted
¼ cup (100g) Orange Purée (*see below*)
½ cup Orange Glaze (*see below*)
6 Candied Kumquat slices, for garnish (*see page 93*)

Preheat oven to 375° and line a 6-cup muffin tin with muffin liners. Sift flour, sugar, brown sugar, baking powder, baking soda, and salt into a large bowl. Add poppyseeds and set aside.

In the bowl of a stand mixer fitted with the whisk attachment, combine eggs, sour cream, and vanilla extract on low speed until fully incorporated. Drizzle in melted butter and whisk on low speed until combined. Add orange purée and mix on low speed until combined.

Add dry ingredients and mix on low speed until just incorporated but no longer, about 30 seconds. Do not overmix. Some dry bits are okay. Remove bowl from stand mixer. Fold in remaining dry bits with a rubber spatula.

Fill each muffin mold ⅔ full. Bake 15 minutes, rotate muffin tin, and continue baking until a toothpick comes out clean, about 12 more minutes. Let muffins cool for 10 minutes. Top each muffin with 1 tablespoon orange glaze and garnish with a slice of candied kumquat.

Orange Purée

Quarter a whole, unpeeled medium Valencia orange and place in food processor. Purée into a coarse paste. Orange Purée can be stored in a freezer bag up to 3 months in the freezer.

Orange Glaze

1 cup (125g) powdered sugar
2 tablespoons orange juice
Water, if needed

Place powdered sugar in the bowl of a stand mixer fitted with the paddle attachment. Mix on low speed, gradually adding orange juice. Consistency will be that of thick glue. Add water by the teaspoon to adjust consistency, if necessary.

BLUEBERRY BRAN MUFFINS

The ever-popular bran muffin, made even more delicious with blueberries.

Makes 6

1/2 cup (112g) buttermilk
1/2 cup (106g) golden brown sugar, packed
1 1/2 cups (92g) wheat bran
1 cup (120g) all-purpose flour
1 teaspoon baking powder
1 teaspoon baking soda
1 teaspoon sea salt
1 large egg, room temperature
1 egg white, room temperature
1/2 cup (100g) grapeseed oil
1 1/4 cups (250g) Golden Raisin Purée (see below)
3/4 cup (120g) frozen blueberries
1/4 cup (55g) turbinado sugar, for sprinkling

Preheat oven to 375° and line a 6-cup muffin tin with muffin liners. In the bowl of a stand mixer fitted with the paddle attachment, combine buttermilk, brown sugar, and wheat bran on low speed for 30 seconds. Scrape bowl well to prevent dry clumps. In a large bowl, combine all-purpose flour, baking powder, baking soda, and salt. Add dry ingredients to buttermilk mixture on low speed.

Stream in egg, egg white, and grapeseed oil and combine on medium-low speed for 30 seconds. Add raisin purée and mix on low speed until just combined. Fold in blueberries.

Fill each muffin mold 2/3 full and sprinkle with turbinado sugar. Bake, rotating pan halfway through, until a toothpick comes out clean, 25 to 28 minutes.

Golden Raisin Purée
1 cup (150g) golden raisins
1/4 cup (55g) water
1/4 teaspoon orange zest

Place raisins, orange zest and water in a small saucepan. Bring to a simmer and simmer for 10 minutes. Remove from heat and cover with plastic wrap to allow raisins to rehydrate. Cool completely. Transfer raisins and liquid to food processor and purée. Let cool and store in a clean, smell-free container in the refrigerator up to 2 weeks.

Tip: Golden Raisin Purée can be made ahead of time. You can store it in the refrigerator for up to two weeks.

Variation: Oat Bran Muffins
This variation on blueberry bran muffins makes oat lovers very happy.

Replace wheat bran with 1 1/3 cups (149g) oat bran. Add 1/2 cup (50g) old-fashioned rolled oats with buttermilk mixture and follow directions above. Replace blueberries with 2/3 cup (100g) dark raisins and omit turbinado sugar.

PEACH CARDAMOM MUFFINS

This fantastic combination of fresh fruit and earthy, fragrant spice is a summer favorite. Any stone fruit will do.

Makes 6

2 cups (240g) all-purpose flour
1/2 cup (100g) granulated sugar
1/4 cup (53g) golden brown sugar, packed
3/4 teaspoon ground cardamom
1 teaspoon baking powder
1 teaspoon baking soda
1/4 teaspoon sea salt
3 large eggs, room temperature
1/2 cup (120g) sour cream
1 tablespoon vanilla extract
1/2 cup (114g) unsalted butter, melted
1 cup sliced peaches
1/2 cup + 1 tablespoon Crisp Topping (see page 32)

Preheat oven to 375° and line a 6-cup muffin tin with muffin liners.

Sift flour, sugar, brown sugar, cardamom, baking powder, baking soda, and salt into a large bowl and set aside.

In the bowl of a stand mixer fitted with the whisk attachment, combine eggs, sour cream, and vanilla extract on low speed. Drizzle in melted butter and whisk on low speed until combined.

Add dry ingredients and mix on low speed until just incorporated. Do not overmix. Some dry bits are okay. Remove bowl from stand mixer and fold in peach slices using a rubber spatula.

Fill each mold 2/3 full. Top each muffin with 1 1/2 tablespoons crisp topping. Bake 15 minutes, rotate muffin tin, and continue baking until a toothpick comes out clean, about 12 more minutes.

VEGAN CHOCOLATE MUFFINS

Silky, smooth, and chocolaty. What more could you want?
Gluten-free

Makes 6

1 tablespoon flaxseed meal
3 tablespoons hot water
1/2 cup (120g) coconut milk
2 teaspoons apple cider vinegar
3/4 cup (106g) white rice flour
1/4 cup (23g) gluten-free oat flour
3/4 cup (160g) dark brown sugar, packed
1/4 cup (21g) Dutch-processed cocoa powder
1 teaspoon baking powder
1/2 teaspoon baking soda
1/2 teaspoon sea salt
1 teaspoon ground cinnamon
1/4 cup (50g) grapeseed oil
1 teaspoon vanilla extract
3/4 cup (120g) shredded zucchini
1/2 cup (78g) carob chips, plus more for garnish
1/2 cup (111g) water, boiling

Preheat oven to 375° and line a 6-cup muffin tin with muffin liners.

In a small bowl, whisk flaxseed meal and hot water together to make a flax egg. Set aside.

In a medium bowl, whisk coconut milk to re-emulsify the fat and coconut water, because coconut milk tends to separate. Whisk apple cider vinegar into coconut milk. Set aside to curdle, about 5 minutes.

Sift rice flour, oat flour, brown sugar, cocoa powder, baking powder, baking soda, salt, and ground cinnamon into a large bowl.

Add grapeseed oil, vanilla extract, and flax egg to the coconut milk mixture and whisk until combined.

Pour wet mixture into the dry mixture and combine with a rubber spatula until dry ingredients are just incorporated. Stir in the shredded zucchini, 1/2 cup carob chips, and boiling water.

Fill molds 2/3 full. Garnish with a sprinkle of carob chips. Bake 15 minutes, rotate muffin tin, and continue baking until a toothpick comes out clean, about 10 more minutes.

VEGAN GINGER MUFFINS

Our first venture into vegan baking turned out to be a big favorite at the café.

Makes 6

3/4 cup + 1 tablespoon (162g) grapeseed oil
1/4 cup + 2 tablespoons (128g) molasses
3/4 cup (229g) maple syrup
1/4 cup + 2 tablespoons (85g) soy milk
1 1/2 cups (180g) all-purpose flour
1 1/2 teaspoons baking powder
3/4 teaspoon baking soda
1 tablespoon + 1 1/2 teaspoons ground ginger
1 1/2 teaspoons ground cinnamon
1/4 teaspoon + 1/8 teaspoon ground cloves
1/4 teaspoon + 1/8 teaspoon sea salt
2 tablespoons powdered sugar, for dusting

Preheat oven to 375° and line a 6-cup muffin tin with muffin liners.

In the bowl of a stand mixer fitted with the paddle attachment, combine grapeseed oil, molasses, maple syrup, and soy milk and mix on low speed 30 seconds.

Sift flour, baking powder, baking soda, ginger, cinnamon, cloves, and salt into a large bowl and add to wet mixture. Combine on low speed until just combined, 15 to 20 seconds. Finish incorporating dry ingredients with a rubber spatula.

Fill molds 2/3 full. Bake for 15 minutes, rotate muffin tin, and continue to bake until a toothpick comes out clean, about 10 more minutes. Dust with powdered sugar before serving.

HOT CROSS BUNS

Funny little buns dressed for church. We love our recipe—it's tender and not too sweet.

Makes 8

3 tablespoons golden raisins
3 tablespoons chopped dried apricots
½ recipe (775g) Brioche dough *(see page 28)*
All-purpose flour, for dusting
1 teaspoon ground cinnamon
½ teaspoon ground cardamom
¼ teaspoon ground allspice
1 egg, for wash
1 recipe Royal Icing *(see below)*

Preheat oven to 375°. Rehydrate raisins and apricots by placing them in a bowl and adding just enough boiling water to cover. Cover with plastic wrap and set aside until cool.

Remove brioche dough from the refrigerator (if it was frozen, remove it ealier). Lightly dust work surface with flour and place dough on floured surface. Divide dough into 8 equal baseball-size balls. Mix raisins, apricots, cinnamon, cardamom, and allspice together in a small bowl. Place 1½ tablespoons raisin-apricot mixture in the center of each ball of dough. Press fruit mix into dough and gather sides of dough to the center.

Form your hand into a claw around dough and roll dough in a circular motion while using your fingers and thumb to tuck the seams in. The seams should gather on the bottom. This will keep the buns from bursting open from the sides.

Place shaped buns 2 inches apart on a parchment-lined sheet pan. Allow buns to proof in warm place until doubled in size, about 30 minutes. Beat egg and use a pastry brush to lightly coat each bun with egg wash.

Bake, rotating halfway through, until golden brown, about 30 minutes. Set aside to cool 15 minutes before decorating with icing.

Royal Icing
2 cups (250g) powdered sugar
1 teaspoon fresh lemon juice
1 egg white
1 teaspoon water

In a medium bowl, whisk together powdered sugar, lemon juice, and egg white. Add 1 teaspoon water, plus more if needed so the consistency is that of thick glue. Transfer icing into a piping bag with a ¼-inch opening. Pipe an "X" over the top of each bun. Let stand at least 10 minutes to allow icing to dry. Serve.

STICKY BUNS

For hardcore fans of sweet breakfast pastries, this sticky, buttery bun is heaven. You can use any nut you have on hand; walnuts are a great substitution. The schmear-style topping was adapted from our good friend and pastry doula, Clemence Gossett.

Makes 6

1/2 recipe (about 775g) Brioche dough (*see page 28*)
1 cup (213g) golden brown sugar, packed
1 cup (228g) unsalted butter, softened
1 tablespoon + 1 teaspoon honey
1 tablespoon bourbon
1 tablespoon vanilla extract
1 teaspoon ground cinnamon
1 1/2 teaspoons sea salt
All-purpose flour, for dusting
3/4 cup (90g) pecan pieces
1 egg, for wash

Remove brioche dough from refrigerator or freezer and let it come to room temperature.

In the bowl of a stand mixer fitted with the paddle attachment, combine brown sugar, butter, honey, bourbon, vanilla, cinnamon, and salt on low speed. Reserve 3/4 cup of this mixture and set aside.

Line work surface with a sheet of parchment paper. Lightly flour parchment and transfer dough to parchment. Lightly flour dough and roll into a 9" x 12" rectangle.

With a small offset spatula, spread remaining filling mixture evenly from edge to edge of brioche dough. Starting with the 9-inch side, roll dough up like a jelly roll, and press edge gently to close seam. Wrap with parchment paper and place in freezer to firm up, about 15 minutes.

Preheat oven to 375°. Meanwhile, scoop 2 tablespoons of filling into each mold of a 6-cup muffin tin and sprinkle with 1 tablespoon pecan pieces. Place muffin tin in oven to heat the filling until bubbly, 3 to 5 minutes. Remove from oven and set aside to cool.

Remove sticky bun log from freezer and slice into 6 equal portions, each about 2 inches thick. Place each portion into muffin tin with spiral showing. Set aside to proof in a warm place until dough has risen above rims of molds, about 1 hour. Beat egg in a small bowl and use pastry brush to apply egg wash.

Bake, rotating halfway through, until golden brown, about 36 minutes. Let cool 5 minutes. Turn pan upside down to release sticky buns. Be sure to scrape all the pecan and caramelized schmear from the muffin tin and spread onto buns. Serve immediately.

CINNAMON ROLLS

Not your traditional cinnamon roll, these bake up crisp, flaky, and buttery. Make the rolls at least a day in advance to store in the freezer, and you can turn out warm, fresh cinnamon rolls for breakfast in only half an hour. Just be sure to cook them all the way to a dark golden brown.

Makes 8

14″ x 16″ sheet frozen Quick Puff Pastry (*see page 27*)
1/4 cup + 2 tablespoons (76g) unsalted butter, softened
1/2 cup + 1 tablespoon (119g) golden brown sugar, packed
1 tablespoon ground cinnamon
1 small or 1/2 large egg white
1 cup (115g) pecans, chopped

Line a work surface with a large sheet of parchment paper. Place the sheet of frozen puff pastry on the parchment and let it just come to room temperature so it is pliable but not soft.

In the bowl of a stand mixer fitted with the paddle attachment, cream butter on low speed until smooth. In a small bowl, combine brown sugar and cinnamon. Add cinnamon sugar to butter and mix on low speed until incorporated. Scrape bowl well with rubber spatula. Add egg white and mix on low speed until incorporated. Scrape bowl well. Increase speed to medium and continue to mix until light and fluffy.

Scrape the cinnamon filling onto the puff pastry with a rubber spatula. Use a metal bench scraper to spread an even, thin layer of filling from edge to edge of the puff pastry. Drag the bench scraper across the filling to ensure an even thickness. Sprinkle pecans evenly over filling. (See step-by-step photos on the next page.)

Starting from one corner of the 16-inch side of the puff pastry sheet, fold the edge over by 1/2 inch. Continue to work across the puff pastry sheet, folding it in this manner. Tuck the puff pastry so that it is snug, and keep rolling it up. If puff pastry is soft, use the parchment paper to help roll the dough into a log. Press the log seam side down to seal. If dough is very soft, return it to the freezer to chill for 5 minutes before slicing.

Use a chef's knife to slice the log into 8 equal pieces. Press rolls, cut side down, to create "feet" that will prevent the formed cinnamon rolls from falling over. Place rolls 2 inches apart on a parchment-lined sheet pan. Freeze until firm, at least 1 hour but preferably overnight. Unbaked cinnamon rolls may be stored in an airtight container in the freezer up to 1 week.

Preheat oven to 375°. Bake, rotating halfway through, until golden brown, about 30 minutes.

STEP BY STEP: MAKING CINNAMON ROLLS

BRIOCHE RING

A favorite around Easter or the winter holidays, these pull-apart buns are soft and pillowy. The more icing the better!

Serves 8

1/2 recipe (about 775g) Brioche dough *(see page 28)*
All-purpose flour, for dusting
2 tablespoons (28g) unsalted butter, softened
1/2 cup (100g) granulated sugar
1 teaspoon ground cinnamon
1 egg, for wash
Vanilla Bean Glaze *(see page 127)*

Remove brioche dough from freezer and let it come to room temperature. Line work surface with a large sheet of parchment paper. Lightly dust it with flour and transfer dough onto the parchment. Lightly dust dough with flour and roll into a 12" x 18" rectangle that is 1/4 inch thick. Arrange the rectangle so the 18-inch side is in front of you.

With a small offset spatula, spread an even layer of softened butter on the dough. In a small bowl, combine sugar and cinnamon. Spread sugar mixture evenly over buttered dough. (See step-by-step photos on the next page.)

Starting from one corner, begin rolling up the long side of the dough to make a log. Tuck and tightly roll the dough over the cinnamon sugar, like rolling up a jelly roll. Work your way across to the other corner, keeping it snug as you roll, and then travel back to the other side, where you originally started. (Picture eating corn on the cob from one end to the other, and then back again.) It's important to roll the dough tightly, so the foundation is strong and the dough won't unravel later when it is portioned and cut. Lift the parchment paper to help roll the dough up. Press on the seam to make sure it sticks.

Position the brioche log so it is sitting on its seam. Join the two ends of the log together to form a ring. Pinch the seams together. Transfer the ring to a parchment-lined sheet pan and place in the freezer to firm up a bit, about 10 minutes.

Preheat oven to 375°. Remove chilled dough from freezer and, starting 1/2 inch from where the ends of the log meet, use a chef's knife to make a cut 1/4 inch from the center so that the center of the ring is still intact. Make seven more evenly-spaced cuts in the same manner to yield eight cuts in total. Twist each cut dough portion clockwise so the cinnamon sugar swirl is showing.

Set aside to proof in a warm place until doubled in size, about 30 minutes.

Whisk egg in a small bowl to make an egg wash. Use a pastry brush to apply egg wash to entire brioche ring. Bake until dough has risen, about 12 minutes. Rotate pan and continue baking until golden brown and cinnamon sugar bubbles at the edges, about 12 more minutes.

While brioche bakes, make the glaze. Allow brioche ring to cool 10 minutes. Spread glaze on top and serve.

STEP BY STEP: MAKING A BRIOCHE RING

CRANBERRY PECAN COFFEE CAKES

Tart cranberries balance the buttery, sweet, nutty crumble topping to make a yummy morning treat.

Makes one 9" x 13" dish; cut to preferred size

4 large eggs, room temperature
1 1/2 cups (340g) sour cream
1 tablespoon vanilla extract
2 1/2 cups + 2 tablespoons (315g) all-purpose flour, sifted
1 1/2 cups (300g) granulated sugar
1 tablespoon baking powder
3/4 teaspoon baking soda
3/4 teaspoon sea salt
3/4 cup (171g) unsalted butter, softened
1 recipe Streusel (see *below*)
1/2 cup (130g) cranberries, fresh or frozen, roughly chopped
1/2 cup (58g) pecan pieces
1 1/2 cups Crisp Topping (see *page 32*)

Preheat oven to 375°. Coat a 9" x 13" baking pan with nonstick spray. In a medium bowl, whisk together eggs, sour cream, and vanilla. Set aside.

In the bowl of a stand mixer fitted with the paddle attachment, combine flour, sugar, baking powder, baking soda, and salt on low speed. Add butter and half of sour cream mixture. Cream on low speed until mixture resembles wet sand, 1 to 2 minutes. Scrape bowl well with a rubber spatula. Add remaining sour cream mixture in 2 additions, scraping the bowl well after each addition. Increase speed to medium and cream until batter is light and fluffy.

Pour 1/3 of batter into prepared dish. Sprinkle 1 cup streusel evenly over batter. Add another 1/3 of batter and 1 cup streusel. Pour remaining batter on top, and sprinkle cranberries and pecans evenly over batter. Cover with remaining streusel and crisp topping.

Bake, rotating halfway through, until a toothpick comes out clean, about 1 hour.

Streusel
3/4 cup (90g) all-purpose flour
3/4 cup (150g) granulated sugar
1/2 cup (106g) golden brown sugar, packed
2 tablespoons ground cinnamon
2 tablespoons unsalted butter, cut into 1/4-inch cubes and chilled

In the bowl of a stand mixer fitted with the paddle attachment, mix flour, sugar, brown sugar, cinnamon, and butter on low speed until combined. Transfer to a large bowl and set aside.

Maplenut

MAPLE OAT SCONES

Lennie LaGuire took the helm in the pastry kitchen one day and made this delicious scone for us. Ever since then, it's been a staple on our menu in the fall and winter.

Makes 16

4 cups (480g) all-purpose flour, plus more for dusting
1 cup (113g) whole-wheat flour
2 cups (198g) old-fashioned rolled oats
1 tablespoon + 2 teaspoons baking powder
1 tablespoon + 1 teaspoon granulated sugar
1 1/2 teaspoons sea salt
2 cups (456g) unsalted butter, cut into 1/4-inch cubes and chilled
4 large eggs
1/2 cup (112g) buttermilk
1/2 cup (156g) maple syrup

Maple Glaze

2 cups (250g) powdered sugar
4 tablespoons grade B maple syrup
2 tablespoons water

In the bowl of a stand mixer fitted with the paddle attachment, combine flours, oats, baking powder, sugar, and salt on the lowest speed. Gradually add butter on low speed and mix until pea-size lumps form.

Add eggs, buttermilk, and maple syrup. Mix on lowest speed until just combined, about 30 seconds. Do not overmix. Dough should be shaggy with some dry bits.

Transfer dough onto a lightly floured surface and pat into a 1-inch-thick rectangle. Cut scones with a 3-inch round cutter. Transfer scones onto a parchment-lined sheet pan with 1 inch of space between each scone. Freeze until firm, at least 1 hour.

Preheat oven to 375°. Bake, rotating halfway through, until golden brown, about 30 minutes.

Meanwhile, make glaze. In the clean, dry bowl of a stand mixer fitted with the paddle attachment, combine powdered sugar, maple syrup, and water on low speed until mixture is smooth and lump-free. Consistency should be that of thick glue. Glaze can be made ahead of time; you can store in an airtight container in the refrigerator for up to 2 weeks. If refrigerated, remove and leave on the counter for 30 minutes to come to room temperature before using.

Spread 1 teaspoon glaze on each warm scone before serving.

HONEY LAVENDER SCONES

Delicate, floral lavender and warm, fragrant honey make a perfect sweet treat.

Makes 14

3/4 cup + 2 tablespoons (210g) heavy whipping cream

3 teaspoons dried lavender buds, divided

4 1/2 cups (540g) all-purpose flour, plus more for dusting

2 teaspoons baking powder

1/2 teaspoon baking soda

1 cup (200g) granulated sugar

1 teaspoon sea salt

3/4 cup (171g) unsalted butter, cut into 1/4-inch cubes and chilled

1 large egg

1/2 cup (112g) buttermilk

1/4 cup lavender buds, for garnish

Honey Glaze

2 cups (250g) powdered sugar

1/4 cup (72g) orange-blossom honey

2 tablespoons water

Preheat oven to 375°. Place cream in a small saucepan over medium heat and scald. Remove from heat and add 1 1/2 teaspoons lavender buds. Cover to infuse for 10 minutes. Strain lavender cream. Discard buds and set cream aside.

In the bowl of a stand mixer fitted with the paddle attachment, combine flour, baking powder, baking soda, sugar, salt, and 1 1/2 teaspoons lavender buds on lowest speed. Gradually add butter and mix on low speed until pea-size lumps form.

Add egg, buttermilk and lavender cream, mixing on lowest speed for 15 to 20 seconds until just combined. Do not overmix. Dough should be shaggy with some dry bits. Transfer onto a lightly floured surface and pat dough into a 1-inch-thick rectangle. Cut scones with a 3-inch round cutter.

Transfer scones onto a parchment-lined sheet pan with 1 inch of space between each scone. Freeze until firm, at least 1 hour.

Bake, rotating halfway through, until golden brown, about 30 minutes.

While scones bake, make honey glaze. Place powdered sugar in the bowl of a stand mixer fitted with the paddle attachment. Mix on low speed, streaming in honey and water. Continue to mix on low speed until glaze is smooth and lump-free and consistency is that of thick glue. This can be made ahead; you can store it in an airtight container in the refrigerator for up to 2 weeks.

Remove glaze from refrigerator and leave it on the counter for 30 minutes to come to room temperature before glazing scones. Spread 1 teaspoon glaze on each warm scone and sprinkle with lavender buds before serving.

PEACH RICOTTA SCONES

Summer peaches and creamy ricotta, plus buttery pastry! You can substitute plums or nectarines.

Makes 16

5 1/2 cups (660g) cake flour
1/2 cup (100g) granulated sugar
2 teaspoons sea salt
2 tablespoons baking powder
1 1/2 cups (342g) unsalted butter, cut into 1/4-inch cubes and chilled
1 cup (240g) heavy whipping cream
4 medium yellow peaches, sliced 1/4 inch thick and frozen
All-purpose flour, for dusting
3/4 cup (168g) whole-milk ricotta
1/2 vanilla bean, split lengthwise and scraped
1 tablespoon granulated sugar
1/4 teaspoon almond extract
2 medium yellow peaches, sliced 1/4 inch thick, for garnish
1/3 cup (67g) granulated sugar, for sprinkling

In the bowl of a stand mixer fitted with the paddle attachment, combine cake flour, sugar, salt, and baking powder on lowest speed. Gradually add butter, mixing on low speed until pea-size lumps form.

Gradually add cream on low speed until the mixture just comes together. You may not need the entire amount. Add frozen peach slices and mix until just combined.

Transfer dough onto a lightly floured surface. Gently pat dough to form a 12-inch square that is 1 inch thick. With a chef's knife, cut dough into 3-inch squares.

Transfer scones onto a parchment-lined sheet pan with 1 inch of space between each scone. Press down on the center of each scone with your thumb to make a divot for the ricotta cream.

In a medium bowl, use a rubber spatula to combine ricotta, vanilla bean seeds, sugar, and almond extract. Place 1 tablespoon of ricotta cream in the center of each scone. Garnish with a slice of peach set off to the side of the ricotta cream. Generously sprinkle sugar on top of the scones. Place in freezer to chill at least 1 hour before baking.

Preheat oven to 375°. Bake 15 minutes, rotate pan, and continue baking until ricotta cream is golden brown and peach slices blister, about 15 more minutes. Cool 10 minutes and serve.

Tip: To split a vanilla bean pod, take the tip of a paring knife and run it down the center. Split one end open and hold it down against a flat surface with thumb and index finger. Then take the blade of paring knife and scrape along the split pod to extract the seeds. As we note in the Mise en Place chapter, splitting beans is easier if you soak them in vanilla extract first—a win-win!

PLUM GINGER SCONES

A great combination of flavors: spicy ginger and tart-but-sweet plum.

Makes 16

5 ½ cups (600g) cake flour
½ cup (100g) granulated sugar
2 teaspoons sea salt
2 tablespoons baking powder
1½ cups (342g) unsalted butter, cut into ¼-inch cubes and chilled
1 cup (240g) heavy whipping cream
¾ cup (90g) candied ginger, chopped
6 Santa Rosa or other dark-skinned plums, sliced ½ inch thick, frozen
1 egg, for wash
⅓ cup (67g) granulated sugar, for sprinkling
Plum Ginger Glaze (see below)

In the bowl of a stand mixer fitted with the paddle attachment, combine cake flour, sugar, salt, and baking powder on lowest speed. Gradually add butter, mixing until pea-size lumps form. Gradually add cream on low speed until mixture just comes together. You may not need the entire amount. Add candied ginger and frozen plum slices and mix until combined.

Form dough into 16 mounds by cupping them between your hands. Flatten each mound with the heel of your hand so it forms a hockey puck shape. Transfer scones to a parchment-lined sheet pan with 1 inch of space between each scone.

Whisk egg in a small bowl to make wash. Use a pastry brush to apply egg wash to the tops of the scones. Sprinkle sugar generously on top of each. Place in freezer to chill for at least 1 hour before baking. While scones are chilling, make glaze.

Preheat oven to 375°. Bake, rotating halfway through, until tops of scones are golden brown, about 30 minutes. Spread 1 tablespoon glaze on each scone and serve.

Plum Ginger Glaze

1 Santa Rosa or dark-skinned plum, sliced into ½-inch-thick pieces
½ cup (111g) water
1 tablespoon granulated sugar
2 cups (250g) powdered sugar
1-inch knob ginger root, grated

Place plum slices, water, and sugar in a small saucepan over medium heat. Bring to a boil. Once plum slices are soft and syrup has turned magenta, remove from heat and strain liquid into a medium bowl. Discard plum slices.

Place powdered sugar in the bowl of a stand mixer fitted with the paddle attachment. Add ¼ cup plum syrup and grated ginger. Mix on lowest speed until mixture comes together and is smooth. Consistency should be that of thick glue. If glaze is too thick, add more plum syrup 1 tablespoon at a time until liquid is fully absorbed. Store in an airtight container in the refrigerator up to 2 weeks. Remove glaze from refrigerator and allow to come to room temperature for 30 minutes before glazing scones.

STRAWBERRY BASIL SCONES

Choose sweet and fragrant berries and basil.

Makes 16

4 ¼ cups (510g) all-purpose flour, plus more for dusting
½ cup (100g) granulated sugar
1 tablespoon + 1 teaspoon baking powder
2 teaspoons sea salt
1½ cups (342g) unsalted butter, cut into ¼-inch cubes and chilled
4 large eggs, cold
½ cup (120g) heavy whipping cream
2 cups (300g) quartered and frozen strawberries
½ cup basil, roughly chopped

In the bowl of a stand mixer fitted with the paddle attachment, combine flour, sugar, baking powder, and salt on lowest speed. Add butter and mix on low speed until pea-size lumps form. Add eggs and cream. Mix on lowest speed until just combined, about 30 seconds.

Add strawberries and basil and mix until just combined. Do not overmix. Dough should be shaggy with some dry bits.

Transfer dough onto a lightly floured surface and pat into a 9″ x 12″ rectangle that is 1 inch thick. Using a chef's knife, cut dough into 3 equal 4-inch-wide sections. Cut each section into 4-inch-long, 3-inch-wide triangles. Transfer scones onto parchment-lined sheet pan with 1 inch of space between each scone. Freeze until firm, at least 1 hour.

Preheat oven to 375°. Bake, rotating halfway through, until golden brown, about 30 minutes.

Tip: Strawberry season begins in May and is in full swing by June. At the café, we take advantage of farmers' market strawberries by freezing the Camarosa or Gaviota varietals after hulling and quartering so we'll have strawberries into the fall. Frozen strawberries also hold up much better than fresh when mixing into scone dough.

STRAWBERRY ROSE SCONES

The rose essence adds a floral note to this beautiful berry scone. You can use blackberry and mulberry, too!

Makes 16

4 1/4 cups (510g) all-purpose flour, plus more for dusting
1/2 cup (100g) granulated sugar
1 tablespoon + 1 teaspoon baking powder
2 teaspoons sea salt
1 1/2 cups (342g) unsalted butter, cut into 1/4-inch cubes and chilled
4 large eggs, cold
1/2 cup (120g) heavy whipping cream
1/2 teaspoon rosewater
2 cups (300g) quartered and frozen strawberries

Strawberry Rose Glaze
2 tablespoons strawberries, quartered
2 cups (250g) powdered sugar
1 teaspoon rosewater

In the bowl of a stand mixer fitted with the paddle attachment, combine flour, sugar, baking powder, and salt on lowest speed. Add butter and mix on low speed until pea-size lumps form. Add eggs, cream, and rosewater. Mix on lowest speed until just combined, 15 to 20 seconds. Add strawberries and mix until just combined, 5 to 10 seconds. Do not overmix. Dough should be shaggy with some dry bits.

Transfer dough onto a lightly floured surface and pat into a 9" x 12" rectangle that is 1 inch thick. Using a chef's knife, cut dough into 3 equal 4-inch-wide sections. Cut each section into 4-inch-long, 3-inch-wide triangles. Transfer scones onto parchment-lined sheet pan with 1 inch of space between each scone. Freeze until firm, at least 1 hour.

Preheat oven to 375°. Bake, rotating halfway through, until golden brown, about 30 minutes.

While scones bake, make the glaze. Place strawberries in small saucepan over medium heat and cook until soft, 3 to 5 minutes. Remove from heat and smash strawberries with a wooden spoon. Combine smashed strawberries, powdered sugar, and rosewater in the bowl of a clean, dry stand mixer fitted with the paddle attachment. Mix on low speed until well incorporated. Consistency will be that of thick glue.

Spread 1 tablespoon strawberry rose glaze on each warm scone and serve.

CURRY PINEAPPLE SCONES

Cecilia was inspired to create these scones by Singapore rice noodles. The flavor combinations are close to her childhood memories.

Makes 16

½ cup (100g) candied pineapple
½ cup (75g) golden raisins
1-inch knob ginger root, peeled and sliced ¼ inch thick
1 cup (222g) water
4 ¼ cups (510g) all-purpose flour, plus more for dusting
2 tablespoons granulated sugar
2 teaspoons sea salt
1 tablespoon + 1 teaspoon baking powder
2 ¼ teaspoons Madras curry powder
1 ½ cups (342g) unsalted butter, cut into ¼-inch cubes and chilled
4 large eggs
¾ cup (180g) heavy whipping cream
Curry Glaze *(see below)*

Combine candied pineapple, raisins, and sliced ginger in a small saucepan over medium heat. Cover with water and bring to a simmer. Remove from heat and cover to rehydrate fruit. Set aside to cool.

Strain fruit and set aside, discarding ginger. Return liquid to a small saucepan over medium heat and cook until reduced to ¼ cup. Consistency should be that of maple syrup. Set aside syrup for use in glaze.

In the bowl of a stand mixer fitted with the paddle attachment, combine flour, sugar, salt, baking powder, and curry powder on lowest speed. Gradually add butter, mixing on low speed until pea-size lumps form. Gradually add eggs and cream on low speed until dough just comes together. Add rehydrated pineapple and raisins on low speed until just combined. Dough should be dry and shaggy.

Transfer dough onto a lightly floured surface. Gently pat dough to a 1-inch thickness. Cut scones with a 3-inch round cutter. Dough scraps can be gently pushed together to form more scones. Transfer scones onto a parchment-lined sheet pan with 1 inch of space between them. Freeze 1 hour before baking.

Preheat oven to 375°. Bake 15 minutes, rotate pan, and continue baking until tops are golden brown and raisins puff up, about 15 more minutes. Cool 5 minutes, spread 1 tablespoon glaze on each scone, and serve.

Curry Glaze

1 ½ cups (188g) powdered sugar
1 teaspoon Madras curry powder
⅛ teaspoon sea salt
¼ cup ginger syrup

In the dry, clean bowl of a stand mixer fitted with the paddle attachment, combine powdered sugar, curry powder, and salt on lowest speed. Drizzle in ginger syrup, continuing to mix on low speed until glaze is smooth and reaches the consistency of thick glue. Glaze can be made ahead of time: store in an airtight container in the refrigerator up to 2 weeks. Let refrigerated glaze come to room temperature on the counter 30 minutes before topping scones.

OATCAKES

This satisfying little cake is also packed with fiber. The flaxseeds, oats, and carrots add beautiful color and crunch. We have to make sure there's one left every day at 4 p.m. for Mr. Bruce Drucker!

Makes 6

1 3/4 cups (173g) old-fashioned rolled oats, divided
1 medium carrot, peeled and shredded
1 cup + 2 tablespoons (135g) all-purpose flour
6 tablespoons (60g) semolina
3 tablespoons golden brown sugar
1 1/8 teaspoons baking soda
1 1/2 teaspoons sea salt
1/2 cup + 2 tablespoons (142g) unsalted butter, cut into 1/4-inch cubes and chilled
1/4 cup + 2 tablespoons (56g) dark raisins
3 tablespoons flaxseeds, whole
1/4 cup + 2 tablespoons (84g) buttermilk
1/4 cup + 2 tablespoons (108g) honey
1 large egg, for wash

Preheat oven to 375°. Lightly coat a 6-cup muffin pan with nonstick spray.

Place 1 1/2 cups (148g) oats and shredded carrot in a food processor and process into a coarse meal. In the bowl of a stand mixer fitted with the paddle attachment, combine oat-carrot mixture, flour, semolina, brown sugar, baking soda, and salt on low speed.

Add butter and mix on low speed until pea-size lumps form, about 1 minute. Add dark raisins and flaxseeds and mix to combine, about 30 seconds. Add buttermilk and honey and mix until just incorporated. Do not overmix. Dough should be shaggy with some dry bits.

Spoon 1/2 cup dough into each muffin mold. Avoid pressing down on dough: leave it craggy. In a small bowl, beat egg and use a pastry brush to apply wash on top of each oatcake. Sprinkle each cake with a few of the remaining oats.

Bake, rotating halfway through, until golden brown, about 30 minutes. Let cool 5 minutes before unmolding. Allow oatcakes to cool, unmolded, upside down so that exterior will be crunchier.

CAKES, TARTS & PIES

I was invited to dinner in Montmartre by an old friend of my mother's. I took the bus, found her apartment, and spent the evening with her family. I will always remember her coming in from work with one cloth bag of groceries: a baguette, a piece of cheese, two bottles of wine, fresh greens and herbs, and a piece of meat wrapped in paper.

I sat in the kitchen while she unpacked her bag and prepared a delicious and simple meal. This meal included cake. She never measured, except with her hand—she just scooped the flour and sugar, poured some milk, and broke an egg. Into the oven, *et voilà*! The most wonderful French pound cake, called *quatre-quarts* (four-fourths), so easily prepared and warm from the oven.

Keeping it simple and accessible, having a few special recipes at hand, turning fruit into crisps or tarts, and scooping flour or sugar with your hand makes it easier to keep a lovely treat on the counter. Cakes don't need to be elaborately decorated, iced, or filled. Add some poached or sugared fruit or a drizzle of honey. Keep it simple and keep baking. Oh, and bake for yourself! If we're always trying to impress someone else, then we often fall short. Bake from your heart, know that food is imperfect, and enjoy the sheer pleasure of making something.

OLIVE OIL CAKE

Clearly we don't like dry cake here at Little Flower. The moistness of this cake means it will keep on the counter for a week—but good luck keeping it that long!

Makes one 9-inch cake

2 cups (240g) all-purpose flour
1 3/4 cups (350g) granulated sugar
1 1/2 teaspoons sea salt
1/2 teaspoon baking soda
1/2 teaspoon baking powder
3 eggs
1 1/4 cups (250g) extra-virgin olive oil
1 1/4 cups (294g) whole milk
1/2 cup (110g) fresh orange juice
1 tablespoon orange zest
Brown Butter Buttercream (*see below*)
Candied Kumquats (*see below*)

Preheat oven to 375°. Line a 9-inch-round, 3-inch-tall cake pan with parchment paper and lightly coat with nonstick spray. Sift together flour, sugar, salt, baking soda, and baking powder and set aside.

In the bowl of a stand mixer fitted with the whisk attachment, beat eggs on medium speed. Stream in olive oil and continue whisking until mixture thickens slightly, 2 to 3 minutes. Stream in milk and orange juice and mix until just combined. Add orange zest. Add dry ingredients on low speed until just combined, about 30 seconds. Use a rubber spatula to scrape bowl to ensure all dry ingredients are incorporated. Batter will look similar to pancake batter.

Pour batter into prepared pan. Bake until cake begins to dome, about 30 minutes. Rotate pan and continue baking until top is golden brown and toothpick comes out clean, 30 to 35 minutes. Meanwhile, make buttercream.

Cool cake at least 2 hours before unmolding. Frost with buttercream and decorate with candied kumquats.

Brown Butter Buttercream

1/2 cup (114g) Brown Butter (*see page 32*)
1 1/2 cups + 3 tablespoons (210g) powdered sugar
1/2 teaspoon sea salt
3/4 teaspoon vanilla extract
1 teaspoon heavy whipping cream
1 teaspoon milk

In the bowl of a stand mixer fitted with the paddle attachment, cream brown butter on medium speed. Add powdered sugar and continue to cream until fluffy. Scrape bowl well. Add salt, vanilla extract, cream, and milk and mix until fully incorporated and buttercream is light and fluffy. Transfer to an odor-free container. Use immediately or store in the refrigerator for up to 2 weeks.

Candied Kumquats

These are great as a garnish, spread on a buttered, toasted baguette, or muddled into lemonade.

12 kumquats
3/4 cup (167g) water
1 cup (200g) granulated sugar

Slice kumquats in fourths. Use a toothpick to remove seeds. Place water and sugar in a small saucepan and bring to a boil. Once sugar dissolves, lower the heat to a simmer. Add sliced kumquats and simmer for 1 hour over low heat, stirring occasionally to prevent them from sticking to the bottom of the pan. Once they are translucent and syrup has thickened and set aside to cool. Pour into sterilized container. Candied kumquats will keep in the refrigerator for up to 6 months.

ALMOND ORANGE CAKE

Our dear friend Emily Green used to bring us crates of the most delicious Valencia oranges from her magnificent garden in Altadena. Our wonderful friend Will brought this recipe to Cecilia, and she made it for Emily. Using the whole orange, including the peel and pith, gives this cake a touch of bitterness and more depth of flavor. Plus, the peel is packed with antioxidants. It has become a favorite at the café.
Gluten-free

Makes one 9-inch cake

4 large eggs
2/3 cup + 1 tablespoon (146g) granulated sugar
4 whole Valencia oranges (peel included), puréed
3/4 teaspoon sea salt
1 1/4 teaspoons baking powder
1 1/2 cups (150g) almond meal
1/4 cup (22g) sliced almonds, toasted
Zest of 1 orange
1/4 cup (41g) powdered sugar, for dusting

Preheat oven to 375°. Line a 9-inch-round cake pan with parchment paper and lightly coat with nonstick spray.

In the bowl of a stand mixer fitted with the whisk attachment, whisk eggs and sugar on low speed until combined. Add orange purée. Scrape bowl well. Add salt, baking powder, and almond meal and mix until just incorporated.

Pour batter into prepared pan and place on middle rack. Bake, rotating halfway through, until toothpick comes out clean, about 1 hour.

Let cool at least 2 hours before unmolding. Garnish with toasted almonds, orange zest, and powdered sugar.

TURMERIC ORANGE CAKE

Satisfy your need for a gluten-free sweet treat that's as delicious as it is beautiful. Turmeric lends the glaze its bright yellow color, and it's good for you, too!
Gluten-free

Makes one 9-inch cake

1 cup + 2 tablespoons (256g) unsalted butter, softened, divided
3/4 cup (104g) finely ground cornmeal, plus more for dusting
1 1/4 cups (250g) granulated sugar
4 large eggs
1/2 cup (125g) sour cream
2 teaspoons ground turmeric, plus more for dusting
1 teaspoon baking soda
1 1/2 cups (150g) almond meal or flour
2 whole Valencia oranges (peel included), puréed
Turmeric Glaze (see *below*)

Preheat oven to 375°. Coat a 9-inch-round, 2-inch-tall cake pan with nonstick spray and line with parchment. With a pastry brush, coat lined pan with a thin coat of the 2 tablespoons (28g) softened butter. Dust with cornmeal.

In the bowl of a stand mixer fitted with the paddle attachment, cream 1 cup (228g) butter and sugar on medium speed until mixture is pale and fluffy. Use a rubber spatula to scrape bowl well to prevent butter chunks. Add eggs one at a time on low speed until fully incorporated. Scrape bowl after each addition. Batter should be fluffy.

Add sour cream, ground turmeric, and baking soda on medium-low speed and mix until fully incorporated. Batter will look broken at first, but keep mixing for 5 more minutes.

Add almond meal and 3/4 cup cornmeal and mix until combined. Scrape bowl well to prevent lumps. Add puréed oranges and mix until just incorporated.

Pour batter into prepared pan. Place onto middle rack of oven and bake until batter soufflés up the sides of the pan, about 30 minutes. Rotate pan and continue baking until a toothpick comes out clean, about 30 more minutes. Set aside to cool while you make the glaze.

Run a small offset spatula around side of cake pan to unmold cake. Pour glaze onto center of cooled cake and use small offset spatula to spread glaze to the edge of the cake, letting it drip down the sides. Allow glaze to dry, about 15 minutes. Dust with ground turmeric and serve.

Turmeric Glaze
1 cup (125g) powdered sugar
1/2 teaspoon ground turmeric
2 tablespoons orange juice
Water, optional

In the bowl of a stand mixer fitted with the paddle attachment, combine powdered sugar and ground turmeric on low speed. Add orange juice and mix on low speed until consistency is that of thick glue. Add water if necessary to make the glaze pourable.

Tip: Raw sliced almonds ground fine in a spice or coffee grinder are a great natural substitute for almond meal or almond flour.

BANANA SKILLET CAKE

So beautiful and caramelized. This cake makes for a simple Sunday afternoon dessert.

Makes one 10-inch cake

¼ cup (57g) unsalted butter
¼ cup + 1½ teaspoons (60g) golden brown sugar, packed
1 ¾ cup (350g) granulated sugar, divided
⅛ teaspoon + ½ teaspoon sea salt
3 medium bananas, halved lengthwise
2 large eggs
½ cup (100g) grapeseed oil
2 tablespoons buttermilk
1 teaspoon vanilla extract
3 rmedium ipe bananas, mashed
1¾ cups (210g) all-purpose flour, sifted
1 teaspoon baking soda
¼ teaspoon ground cinnamon

Preheat oven to 350°. Melt butter in a 10-inch cast iron skillet over medium heat. Whisk in ¾ cup (150g) sugar and brown sugar until they dissolve, bubble, and caramelize, 3 to 5 minutes. Remove from heat and set aside to cool. Sprinkle with ⅛ teaspoon salt. Lay bananas cut side-down on caramel. Set aside.

In the bowl of a stand mixer fitted with the whisk attachment, whisk eggs and 1 cup (200g) sugar on medium speed until mixture is light and fluffy and a trail of batter hangs from the whisk for 3 to 5 seconds (ribbon stage). Stream in oil, buttermilk, and vanilla extract on low speed until just combined. Add mashed bananas and mix on low speed until just incorporated. Sift flour, baking soda, ½ teaspoon salt, and cinnamon into wet mixture and mix until just incorporated.

Place skillet onto a sheet pan and pour batter over bananas and caramel. Bake 15 minutes, rotate pan, and continue baking until a toothpick comes out clean, about 15 more minutes. Let cool 5 minutes before inverting onto plate.

PEAR CAKE

Dorie Greenspan has been an inspiration my entire career. I had the honor of meeting her in Paris years ago and will forever treasure the time I had with her. Her apple cake is a favorite. We also love it with ripe fall pears, and so do our customers. Thanks, Dorie!

Makes one 8-inch cake

2 eggs, room temperature
3/4 cup (150g) granulated sugar, plus another 1/4 cup (50g) for sprinkling
1 teaspoon vanilla extract
1/2 cup (114g) unsalted butter, melted
3/4 cup (90g) all-purpose flour, sifted
3/4 teaspoon baking powder
1/8 teaspoon sea salt
4 Bartlett pears, peeled, cored, and roughly chopped

Preheat oven to 375°. Line an 8-inch-round cake pan with parchment paper and lightly coat with nonstick spray.

In the bowl of a stand mixer fitted with the whisk attachment, whisk eggs on medium speed until foamy. Add 3/4 cup (150g) sugar and vanilla extract and continue to whisk on medium speed until thick and pale, about 5 minutes. Scrape bowl well with a rubber spatula. Stream in melted butter and mix until just incorporated. Add flour, baking powder, and salt and mix until just combined. Fold in chopped pears with rubber spatula. Pour batter into prepared pan. Liberally sprinkle remaining sugar on top.

Bake, rotating halfway through, until top of cake is golden brown and flaky and toothpick comes out clean, about 1 hour. Cool 30 minutes before unmolding.

CARROT CAKE

We get a lot of requests for gluten-free desserts. This carrot cake is so delicious that you'd never guess it's any different from the rest.
Gluten-free

Makes one 9-inch, 4-layer cake

2 1/4 cups (450g) granulated sugar
1 cup + 3 tablespoons (253g) golden brown sugar, packed
2 teaspoons orange zest
2 1/2 cups (500g) grapeseed oil
8 large eggs
3 1/3 cups (480g) white rice flour, sifted
1 3/4 cups (160g) gluten-free oat flour, sifted
1 tablespoon + 1 teaspoon baking powder
2 teaspoons baking soda
1 1/2 teaspoons sea salt
2 teaspoons ground cinnamon
2 teaspoons ground ginger
5 cups (500g) shredded carrots
1 3/4 cups (200g) walnuts, coarsely chopped
1 cup (150g) golden raisins
Cream Cheese Frosting *(see next page)*

Preheat oven to 375°. Prepare 4 9-inch-round, 2-inch-tall cake pans by lining with parchment paper and lightly coating with nonstick spray. Set aside.

In the bowl of a stand mixer fitted with the whisk attachment, whisk together sugar, brown sugar, orange zest, and oil on medium-low speed until well combined. Add eggs one at a time on low speed, using a rubber spatula to scrape the bowl well after each addition. Increase speed to medium and whisk until fluffy, about 2 minutes. Add rice flour, oat flour, baking powder, baking soda, salt, cinnamon, and ginger and mix on low speed until just incorporated. Fold in carrots, walnuts, and raisins and mix on low speed until just combined, about 15 seconds.

Divide batter evenly between cake pans. Bake for 15 minutes, rotate pans, and continue baking until a toothpick comes out clean, about 15 more minutes. Let cool completely before unmolding. When cool, unmold and coat with cream cheese frosting. (*See instructions for layer-cake assembly on page 30.*)

Cream Cheese Frosting

½ cup (114g) unsalted butter, softened
1 cup (228g) cream cheese, softened
4 cups (500g) powdered sugar
1½ teaspoons vanilla extract

In the bowl of a stand mixer fitted with the paddle attachment, cream butter and cream cheese on medium speed until fluffy, about 2 minutes. Add powdered sugar in 3 additions on low speed. Scrape bowl well with a rubber spatula after each addition. Add vanilla extract and mix until fully incorporated. Scrape bowl well. Use immediately or store in an airtight container in the refrigerator up to 2 weeks.

CHOCOLATE CAKE

The brown butter frosting makes this cake extra flavorful. It's our number-one flavor combination at Little Flower.

Makes one 9-inch, 4-layer cake

2 cups (456g) unsalted butter, softened
4 cups (800g) granulated sugar
4 large eggs, room temperature
2 teaspoons vanilla extract
2 teaspoons almond extract
2 1/2 cups (560g) brewed coffee, room temperature
2 cups (500g) sour cream
5 1/2 cups + 1 tablespoon (684g) all-purpose flour, sifted
2 cups (228g) Dutch-processed cocoa powder, sifted
1 tablespoon + 1 teaspoon baking powder
2 teaspoons baking soda
2 teaspoons sea salt
Brown Butter Buttercream Frosting *(see page 33)*

Preheat oven to 350°. Line two 9-inch-round cake pans with parchment and lightly coat with nonstick spray.

In the bowl of a stand mixer fitted with the paddle attachment, cream butter and sugar on medium speed until fluffy. Use a rubber spatula to scrape bowl well. Add eggs one at a time and mix until well combined. Scrape bowl well after each addition. Add vanilla extract and almond extract and mix on low speed until well combined. Scrape bowl well.

In a medium bowl, whisk coffee and sour cream together. Set aside. In a large bowl, mix together flour, cocoa powder, baking powder, baking soda, and salt. Add dry ingredients and coffee mixture alternately, starting and ending with dry ingredients. Scrape bowl well after each addition. Mix on medium speed until batter is fluffy and smooth, about 1 minute.

Divide batter evenly between cake pans. Bake 20 minutes, rotate pans, and continue baking until cake domes slightly and a toothpick comes out clean, 20 to 25 more minutes. Let cool before unmolding. Wrap each layer with plastic wrap and chill.

Place cake layer on cake turntable. Use a serrated knife to score edge of cake to split it into two even layers. Once scored, use serrated knife in a sawing motion to carefully split the cake. Repeat with the other cake, so you end up with 4 layers. Trim off domes and frost with brown butter buttercream. *(See instructions for layer-cake assembly on page 30.)*

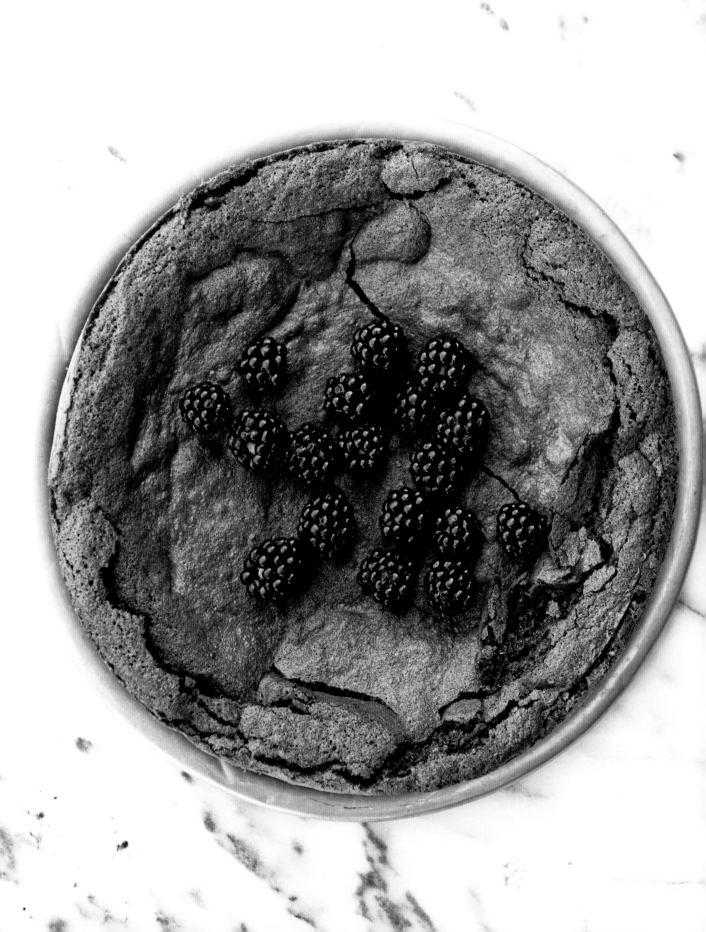

RUSTIC CHOCOLATE CAKE

The crunchy crust and moist middle make this cake a standout. Top it with whipped cream and fruit, or let it stand alone—either way, it's a favorite. It's also an easy dessert to whip up!

Makes one 9-inch cake

1 1/2 cups (250g) chopped bittersweet chocolate, 70% cacao
1/2 cup + 2 tablespoons (142g) unsalted butter, softened
1 1/2 cups (300g) granulated sugar, divided
4 large eggs, separated, room temperature
1 tablespoon vanilla extract
1 1/4 cups (150g) all-purpose flour, sifted
1 teaspoon baking soda
1/4 teaspoon sea salt
1/4 cup (41g) powdered sugar, for dusting

Preheat oven to 350°. Line a 9-inch-round cake pan with parchment paper and lightly coat with nonstick spray.

Fill a medium saucepan halfway with water and place over medium heat. Bring water to a simmer. Place chocolate in mixing bowl and set on top of saucepan. Stir occasionally with a rubber spatula until chocolate has melted. Remove from heat and set aside.

In the bowl of a stand mixer fitted with the paddle attachment, cream butter and 1 cup (200g) sugar on medium speed until fluffy, 2 to 3 minutes. Use a rubber spatula to scrape bowl well. Add egg yolks and vanilla extract and mix on low speed until well combined. Add melted chocolate on low speed until just combined, leaving some streaks. Add flour, baking soda, and salt and mix on low speed until just incorporated. Transfer to large bowl and set aside.

In the dry, clean bowl of a stand mixer fitted with the whisk attachment, whisk egg whites on medium-high speed until frothy. Slowly add 1/2 cup (100g) sugar and whip until medium-soft peaks form, 5 to 8 minutes. Fold meringue into chocolate mixture.

Pour batter into prepared pan. Bake until cake soufflés up the sides of the pan, about 30 minutes. Rotate pan and continue baking until a toothpick comes out clean, 20 to 25 more minutes. Let cool before unmolding. Dust with powdered sugar and serve.

FLOURLESS CHOCOLATE CAKE

So dense and chocolaty that you only need a small sliver. This cake goes a long way!
Gluten-free

Makes one 8-inch cake

2/3 cup (110g) chopped bittersweet chocolate, 70% cacao
1/2 cup (114g) unsalted butter
3/4 cup (150g) granulated sugar
3 large eggs, room temperature
1/2 cup (50g) Dutch-processed cocoa powder, sifted
4-ounce block dark chocolate, frozen

Preheat oven to 375°. Line an 8-inch-round cake pan with parchment paper and lightly coat with nonstick spray.

Combine chocolate and butter in a double boiler or large metal bowl set over a saucepan of simmering water. Stir with a rubber spatula to melt mixture until smooth. Remove from heat and whisk in sugar. Add eggs one at a time, whisking well after each addition. Whisk in cocoa powder until just combined. Pour batter into prepared pan. Bake, rotating halfway through, until top forms a thin crust, about 30 minutes. Allow cake to cool in pan 15 minutes.

Use a vegetable peeler or knife to make chocolate curls from the frozen block of chocolate. Decorate top of cake with chocolate curls.

COCONUT CAKE

Pillowy coconut cake, how beautiful and moist you are! Any day is a good day for coconut cake.

Makes one 9-inch, 4-layer cake

1 recipe Perfect White Cake, baked *(see page 29)*
1 1/4 cups (300g) heavy whipping cream
3/4 cup (150g) granulated sugar
1/2 cup (114g) unsalted butter
1 tablespoon cornstarch
1/4 teaspoon vanilla extract
1 teaspoon water
3 3/4 cups (318g) sweetened shredded coconut, divided
Buttercream Frosting or Coconut Buttercream Frosting *(see page 33)*

Combine cream, sugar, and butter in a medium saucepan over medium heat and bring to a boil. Stir constantly until sugar is dissolved. Meanwhile, in a small bowl, combine cornstarch, vanilla extract, and water to make a slurry. Add to cream mixture, stirring constantly. Bring to a boil and simmer until mixture thickens, about 1 minute. Remove from heat.

Place 2 1/4 cups (191g) shredded coconut in food processor and pulse until finely chopped. Fold coconut into cream mixture. Transfer coconut filling to a container and let cool. Chill in the refrigerator overnight. Coconut filling may be stored in the refrigerator up to 2 weeks.

Just before using, place coconut filling in the bowl of a stand mixer fitted with the paddle attachment, and beat until smooth and creamy, 3 to 4 minutes.

Follow layer cake assembly directions *(see page 30)*. Fill layers with coconut filling and frost with buttercream frosting or coconut buttercream. After applying the final coat of frosting, cover cake with remaining 1 1/2 cups (127g) shredded coconut.

MILK & HONEY CAKE

Cecilia and I developed this cake for my brother Jim's fiftieth birthday. He loves dulce de leche, so we used those flavors to create this sweet treat. Best served icy cold in a shallow bowl, this mouthwatering cake will make everyone happy. This is a year-round crowd-pleaser, so swap the plums for other fruit if they're not in season.

Serves 12

Milk Reduction
Make at least 1 day before you assemble the cake. Can be made up to 2 days in advance.

6 cups (1410g) whole milk
¼ cup (72g) buckwheat honey or raw honey

Place milk in saucepan and bring to a simmer. Continue reducing at a simmer for 30 minutes. Add honey and continue to simmer for another 30 minutes. The reduction will have a light caramel color. Cool completely and remove any skin that has developed, or strain.

Sheet Cake
Make at least 1 day before you assemble the final cake, so it has time to soak in the Milk Reduction overnight.

5 large eggs, separated, room temperature
1 cup (200g) granulated sugar, divided
1 teaspoon vanilla extract
½ cup (114g) unsalted butter, melted and cooled
1½ cups (180g) all-purpose flour, sifted
1 teaspoon baking powder
½ teaspoon sea salt
1 recipe Milk Reduction (see recipe above)

Preheat oven to 350°. Lightly coat a half-sheet cake pan with nonstick spray and line with parchment paper.

In the bowl of a stand mixer fitted with the whisk attachment, whisk egg yolks on high speed until foamy. Rain in ½ cup (100g) sugar and whisk until mixture reaches the ribbon stage, about 5 minutes. Add the vanilla extract and melted butter and whisk until just incorporated. Set aside.

In the clean, dry bowl of a stand mixer fitted with the whisk attachment, whisk egg whites on high speed until foamy. Rain in remaining ½ cup (100g) sugar and whisk until meringue is medium-stiff, 5 to 8 minutes. Check consistency by dipping a spoon into the meringue. When lifted, a peak resembling a bird's beak should form.

Gently fold ½ cup meringue into yolk mixture with a rubber spatula to loosen batter. Add remaining meringue and gently fold in with a balloon whisk: drag whisk through center of bowl and up sides, and then rotate bowl 90 degrees. Continue folding in this manner until just incorporated but no more. There should be some streaks of meringue left. Sift together flour, baking powder, and salt into a large bowl. Fold sifted dry ingredients into the batter until just incorporated.

Pour batter into prepared pan. Use an offset spatula to spread batter evenly. Bake, rotating halfway through, until a toothpick comes out clean, about 12 minutes. Let cool. Invert and remove parchment paper, and then return cake to pan. Set aside 1 cup milk reduction for the final assembly and slowly pour the rest over cake to soak overnight. Wrap tightly with plastic wrap and chill in the refrigerator.

Sea Salt Caramel Sauce

1/2 cup (120g) heavy whipping cream
1/4 pound (1/2 cup, or 114g) sea salt caramels

Place cream in saucepan and bring to a simmer. Add caramels and whisk until caramels dissolve. Remove from heat and store in container until ready to assemble.

Honey Cream

4 cups (960g) heavy whipping cream
1/4 cup (72g) buckwheat honey or raw honey

In the bowl of a stand mixer fitted with the whisk attachment, whisk cream on high speed until medium-soft peaks form. Add honey and mix until just incorporated. Store in the refrigerator until ready to assemble.

Plum Compote

10 Santa Rosa or other dark-skinned plums, each sliced into 10 wedges
1 tablespoon bourbon
1 vanilla bean, split lengthwise and scraped
1/2 cup (100g) granulated sugar
1/4 teaspoon sea salt

Place 3/4 of the plum slices, bourbon, vanilla bean and seeds, sugar, and salt in a medium saucepan over medium heat. Stir with a rubber spatula to make sure plums are well coated. Bring mixture to a simmer, stirring occasionally, until plums have softened and juices are released. Continue to simmer until mixture forms a thick sauce, about 30 minutes. Strain and discard plum skins and vanilla bean pod. Cool compote completely. Store sauce in an airtight container in the refrigerator. Toss remaining plum wedges into chilled sauce before serving.

Assembly

Sheet Cake (*see page 113*)
1 cup Milk Reduction (*see page 113*)
1 recipe Sea Salt Caramel Sauce (*see recipe above*)
1 recipe Honey Cream (*see recipe above*)
1 recipe Plum Compote (*see recipe above*)

Cut cake in half. Transfer one half to a 9" x 13" baking dish. Drizzle 1/2 cup milk reduction over cake. Spread 3 cups honey cream evenly on top of cake. Drizzle 1/4 cup caramel sauce over cake. Top with remaining cake half and repeat layering process. Use a serving spoon to scoop a portion onto bowl or plate. Spoon plum compote on the side and top with additional honey cream and a drizzle of caramel sauce. Serve.

Tips: Take the time to reduce your milk slowly, because it will develop the sugars. And remember that you need to make the sheet cake, milk reduction, and plum compote a day before you assemble the cake.

ROYAL BISCUIT CAKE

This was Prince William's groom's cake. We substitute graham crackers for digestive cookies.

Makes one 9-inch cake

2 cups (340g) chopped bittersweet chocolate, 70% cacao, divided
1 cup (170g) chopped unsweetened chocolate
1 1/2 cups (360g) heavy whipping cream, divided
1/2 cup (114g) unsalted butter, softened
1 cup (200g) granulated sugar
3 large eggs, room temperature
4 3/4 cups (410g) graham crackers, coarsely crushed
1/2 cup Sea Salt Caramel Sauce (*see page 33*)
1/2 teaspoon sea salt

Place a 9-inch cake ring on a parchment-lined sheet pan. Cut a 3-inch-wide rectangular strip of parchment paper to create a collar for the sides of the cake ring. Lightly coat parchment paper with nonstick spray.

To make the ganache, place 1 cup (170g) bittersweet chocolate, unsweetened chocolate, and 1/2 cup (120g) cream in a double boiler or metal bowl over a saucepan of simmering water. Stir occasionally with a rubber spatula until chocolates have melted and mixture is smooth. Remove ganache from heat and set aside.

In the bowl of a stand mixer fitted with the paddle attachment, cream butter and sugar on medium-low speed until light and fluffy. Add ganache on low speed until well combined. Add eggs one at a time, scraping bowl well with a rubber spatula after each addition. Remove bowl from stand mixer and fold in graham cracker pieces with rubber spatula, making sure pieces are well coated with chocolate mixture. Pour half of biscuit mixture into prepared cake pan. Spread a thin layer of sea salt caramel sauce on top. Cover with remaining biscuit mixture. Gently press down to remove any air gaps. Chill cake in the refrigerator at least 3 hours.

Make a second batch of ganache: Place cream in small saucepan and bring to a scald. Place 1 cup (170g) bittersweet chocolate in a mixing bowl. Pour 1 cup (240g) cream over chocolate and let sit for 2 to 3 minutes. Add salt and stir with rubber spatula until ganache is smooth.

Remove cake from refrigerator. Unmold cake upside-down and set on a cooling rack. Pour ganache over cake and use an offset spatula to smooth the top and sides. Allow ganache to set before serving.

LEMON SEMOLINA CAKES

These delicate-yet-sturdy individual cakes get a good soak of delicious lemony syrup. They'll last for days in an airtight container, even after soaking.

Makes 6 large, muffin-size cakes

3/4 cup (90g) all-purpose flour
1/2 cup + 2 tablespoons (102g) semolina
1 1/2 teaspoons baking powder
3/4 teaspoon sea salt
3 large eggs
3/4 cup (150g) granulated sugar
1/2 cup + 1 tablespoon (113g) extra-virgin olive oil
1 tablespoon + 1 1/2 teaspoons fresh lemon juice
1/2 teaspoon lemon zest
Lemon Syrup (*see recipe below*)
Mint Glaze (*see recipe next page*)
Candied Mint (*see recipe next page*)

Preheat oven to 350°. Generously coat a 6-cup muffin tin with nonstick spray.

Sift together flour, semolina flour, baking powder, and salt onto a sheet of parchment paper.

Place eggs in the bowl of a stand mixer fitted with the whisk attachment and whisk on medium speed until foamy. Rain in sugar and whisk on medium-high speed until mixture is pale yellow and has a thick consistency (ribbon stage), 4 to 6 minutes. Slowly pour in olive oil, lemon juice, and lemon zest and mix on medium speed until combined. Lift the two sides of parchment paper and pour sifted dry ingredients into bowl, mixing on low speed until just incorporated.

Divide batter evenly among muffin molds. Bake, rotating halfway through, until a toothpick comes out clean, about 20 minutes. Meanwhile, make lemon syrup.

Let cakes cool 5 minutes. Unmold and dip each in syrup. Place cakes on a cooling rack over a parchment-lined sheet pan, allowing cakes to fully cool and soak up syrup. Invert cakes so the bottom is the top. Spread about 1 tablespoon mint glaze over each cooled cake. Garnish with candied mint and serve.

Lemon Syrup
1/2 cup (100g) granulated sugar
1/2 cup (111g) water
1/4 cup (60g) fresh lemon juice
1 tablespoon lemon zest

Place sugar and water in saucepan and boil until sugar is dissolved. Add lemon juice and zest. Set aside in a shallow bowl to dip cooled cakes.

Tips: An ice cream scoop with a trigger is a handy tool to portion the batter evenly and to scoop it into the muffin tin mess-free. Also note that the syrup and mint garnish can be made a day ahead.

Mint Glaze

Tip: The leftover mint syrup makes a great lemonade!

½ cup (100g) granulated sugar
½ cup (111g) water
1 bunch fresh mint
1½ cups (187g) powdered sugar

Place granulated sugar and water in a saucepan and boil until sugar is dissolved. Remove from heat. Add mint and steep for 15 minutes. Strain and discard mint, retaining the liquid.

Place powdered sugar in bowl of a stand mixer fitted with the paddle attachment. Measure ¼ of the mint syrup and add it to the sugar. Mix on low speed until glaze is smooth. Save the leftover mint syrup for another use.

Candied Mint

1 egg white
6 small mint leaves
2 tablespoons granulated sugar

Whisk egg white with a fork to break up albumen. Use a pastry brush to brush both sides of mint leaves with egg white. Dip each leaf in granulated sugar. Set leaves on a parchment-lined sheet pan to dry overnight, or at least 2 hours.

PLUOT FINANCIER

This classic French cake has captured my heart. I like using almonds with the skin on for color and texture. Add summer plums or pluots bursting with juice and watch how beautifully they come together. Pure heaven.

Makes one 8" x 8" dish; cut to preferred size

1/2 cup (114g) unsalted butter
3/4 cup + 2 tablespoon (90g) almond flour or meal, toasted
1/2 cup (60g) cake flour, sifted
1 1/2 cups (187g) powdered sugar
3 egg whites, room temperature
4 medium pluots, pitted and halved
2 tablespoons granulated sugar

Preheat oven to 375°. Coat an 8" x 8" baking dish with nonstick spray and set aside.

To make brown butter, place butter in a medium saucepan over high heat. Bring to a boil and lower heat to medium. Use a wooden spoon or heat-resistant spatula to stir, scraping any milk solids off bottom of saucepan. The milk solids will continue to brown, yielding the nutty, brown bits of love. Allow butter to foam a second time. Remove from heat and set aside.

In the bowl of a stand mixer fitted with the paddle attachment, combine almond flour, cake flour, and powdered sugar on low speed for 30 seconds. Stream in egg whites on low speed until incorporated, then increase speed to medium and mix 3 minutes. Scrape bowl well.

Decrease speed to low and stream in warm brown butter. Be sure to scrape all the brown bits into the mixing bowl. Mix on low speed for 1 minute, and then increase speed to medium and mix for 3 minutes. Scrape bowl well.

Pour batter into prepared pan. Place pluot halves into batter cut side up. Liberally sprinkle sugar over top of batter and pluots. Bake until batter soufflés up the sides of the pan, about 40 minutes. Rotate pan and continue baking until a toothpick comes out clean, about 40 more minutes.

Tips: To toast the almond flour, spread on a parchment-lined sheet pan and bake in a 375° oven until golden brown, about 5 minutes. If you don't have almond flour, you can toast sliced natural almonds in the oven until golden brown, 8 to 10 minutes, then grind in a food processor.

MICHELLE'S TOMATO RICOTTA CAKE

This creative cake was the winner at a tomato cook-off in Tujunga, outside of L.A. Its creator, my friend Michelle Valigura, was generous enough to share it. We love it and think you will, too.

Makes one 9-inch, 2-layer cake

Tomato Marmalade

6 pounds tomatoes, blanched, peeled, seeded, and quartered
2 cups (400g) granulated sugar
1 cinnamon stick, toasted
1 tablespoon vanilla extract

Place tomatoes, sugar, cinnamon stick, and vanilla extract in a large saucepan. Stir together and simmer over medium-low heat. Stir occasionally to prevent tomatoes from burning. Simmer until tomatoes break down and mixture has the consistency of a thick jam or marmalade, about 1 hour. Cool thoroughly before storing in a covered container in the refrigerator.

Ricotta Cake

3 large eggs
1½ cups (340g) whole-milk ricotta
1 teaspoon vanilla extract
1½ cups (180g) all-purpose flour, sifted
1 cup (200g) granulated sugar
2 teaspoons baking powder
1 teaspoon sea salt
½ cup (114g) unsalted butter, melted

Preheat oven to 350°. Line bottom of 9-inch-round, 3-inch-tall cake pan with parchment and lightly coat with nonstick spray.

In a large bowl, whisk eggs, ricotta, and vanilla extract together until smooth. Add flour, sugar, baking powder, and salt and fold in until just incorporated. Fold in melted butter until just combined.

Pour batter into prepared pan. Bake, rotating halfway through, until toothpick comes out clean, about 1 hour. Cool for 2 hours before unmolding.

Tomato Cream Cheese Frosting

2 tablespoons (28g) unsalted butter, softened
6 tablespoons (113g) cream cheese, softened
¼ teaspoon vanilla extract
1 cup (125g) powdered sugar
1 tablespoon tomato paste
⅛ teaspoon sea salt

In the bowl of a stand mixer fitted with the paddle attachment, cream butter and cream cheese on medium-low speed until smooth and fluffy. Add vanilla extract, powdered sugar, and tomato paste and combine on medium speed until fully incorporated.

Assembly

1 Ricotta Cake
2 cups Tomato Marmalade
½ cup (125g) plain Greek yogurt
Tomato Cream Cheese Frosting

Place ricotta cake layer on cake turntable. Use a serrated knife to score edge of cake to split it into two even layers. Once scored, use serrated knife in a sawing motion to carefully split the cake. Transfer top layer to a 9-inch-round cardboard cake board and set aside.

Use a small offset spatula to spread 2 cups marmalade on bottom layer. Spread yogurt over the marmalade. Gently slide the top layer back on. Gently press to make sure cake layer is secure. Use small offset spatula to frost and decorate cake with tomato cream cheese frosting as desired.

Tips: The tomato marmalade can be made a few days ahead. It's also delicious atop toast or waffles. Summer tomatoes are usually flavorful and gorgeous—taste the tomatoes and adjust the sugar accordingly.

QUINCE SHORTCAKES

The pink-amber color of cooked quince makes this compote a beautiful accompaniment to the tender shortcakes. An irresistible dessert.

Makes 8

2 cups + 2 tablespoons (255g) all-purpose flour, plus more for dusting

2 3/4 teaspoons baking powder

1/2 teaspoon sea salt

1/4 cup (50g) granulated sugar, plus another 1/4 cup (50g) for sprinkling

1/4 cup + 2 tablespoons (86g) unsalted butter, cut into 1/4-inch cubes and chilled

1 cup (240g) heavy whipping cream

1 egg, beaten, for wash

Quince Compote (*see below*)

2 cups heavy cream, whipped to medium-soft peaks

In the bowl of a stand mixer fitted with the paddle attachment, combine flour, baking powder, salt, and sugar on low speed. Gradually add butter and mix until pea-size lumps form, about 2 minutes. Slowly add cream and mix until dough just comes together. Dough should be on the shaggier, dry side. Transfer onto a lightly floured work surface and gently pat into a 1-inch-thick rectangle. Dough will feel tacky and supple but not sticky. Use a 2 1/2-inch cutter to portion shortcakes. Transfer onto a parchment-lined sheet pan. Apply egg wash with pastry brush. Sprinkle sugar over shortcakes. Freeze overnight or up to 2 weeks in airtight container.

Preheat oven to 375°. Bake, rotating halfway, until golden brown, about 24 minutes. Split shortcakes in half. Place quince slices and syrup on bottom halves, add dollops of whipped cream, and top with top halves.

Quince Compote

6 cups (1332g) water

1 cup (200g) granulated sugar

1/4 cup (72g) wildflower honey

1 vanilla bean, split lengthwise and scraped

2 cinnamon sticks, toasted

2 star anise, toasted

3 slices fresh ginger

4 whole quince (1000g)

1 tablespoon fresh lemon juice

Choose a large saucepan and cut a parchment circle with a diameter equal to that of the saucepan. Cut a 1-inch hole in the center of parchment circle and set aside. Combine water, sugar, honey, vanilla bean and seeds, cinnamon sticks, star anise, and ginger slices in the large saucepan over medium heat. Bring poaching liquid to a simmer and reduce heat to low.

Use a small paring knife to quarter quince lengthwise. Lay quartered pieces flat side down and cut at an angle to remove stems, cores, and bottoms. Use a vegetable peeler to remove skin. Immediately place prepared quince quarters into poaching liquid to prevent oxidation.

Place parchment circle directly on top of quince and poaching liquid. This will keep the quince submerged in liquid. Poach quince over low heat until fork-tender. Add lemon juice and stir to combine. (The lemon's acid helps draw out the anthocyanins in quince to turn them a lovely pink.) Remove from heat and let cool in saucepan to infuse quince with spices. Transfer to a container and refrigerate overnight. Quince will darken to a rosy hue.

Strain liquid into a small saucepan, discarding spices and setting quince quarters aside. Reduce quince liquid to a thick syrup. Slice quince quarters into wedges and toss in syrup.

MOOSEHEAD GINGERBREAD

This recipe is from one of my favorite bakers, Maida Heatter. Her books have been staples in my library from the beginning of my career, and her gingerbread has always been a part of my holiday tradition.

Makes one Pullman loaf

½ cup (114g) unsalted butter, softened
½ cup (106g) dark brown sugar, packed
2 large eggs, room temperature
1 cup (340g) molasses
1 tablespoon ground espresso
2 ½ cups (300g) all-purpose flour, sifted
2 teaspoons baking soda
½ teaspoon sea salt
1 teaspoon ground cinnamon
1 ½ teaspoons ground ginger
½ teaspoon ground cloves
½ teaspoon ground mustard
½ teaspoon freshly ground black pepper
1 cup (222g) boiling water
Vanilla Bean Glaze *(see below)*

Preheat oven to 375°. Line a Pullman loaf pan with parchment paper and lightly coat with nonstick spray.

In the bowl of a stand mixer fitted with the paddle attachment, cream butter on low speed until smooth. Add brown sugar and mix on low speed for 2 minutes. Add eggs one at a time and mix until well combined. Scrape bowl well with rubber spatula. Add molasses and espresso and continue mixing until well combined and smooth. Scrape bowl well.

In a large bowl, combine flour, baking soda, salt, cinnamon, ginger, cloves, mustard, and pepper. Add ⅓ of these dry ingredients to the butter-sugar mixture, followed by half the boiling water, mixing on low speed. Add another ⅓ of the dry ingredients, the remaining hot water, and finally the remaining dry ingredients. Mix on low speed until batter is smooth. Scrape bowl well. Pour batter into prepared pan.

Bake, rotating halfway, until a toothpick comes out clean, about 1 hour. Cool cake for 10 minutes before unmolding. Decorate gingerbread with vanilla bean glaze and serve.

Vanilla Bean Glaze

1 cup (125g) powdered sugar
1 vanilla bean, split lengthwise and scraped
¼ cup (56g) water

In the bowl of a stand mixer fitted with the paddle attachment, combine powdered sugar, vanilla bean seeds, and water. Combine on low speed until smooth and thick. Consistency should be that of thick glue. Store in an airtight container until ready to use.

APPLE CRISP

The aroma of baking apples and cinnamon is a classic. Having this crisp topping in your fridge or freezer will ensure you can always throw this together, even at the last minute.

Makes one 9" x 12" dish; cut to preferred size

12 Granny Smith apples, peeled, cored, and sliced 1/4 inch thick
1 tablespoon fresh lemon juice
1/2 cup (100g) granulated sugar, divided
1 tablespoon cornstarch
1/2 teaspoon ground cinnamon
1 tablespoon vanilla extract

Crisp Topping
1 1/2 cups (180g) all-purpose flour
3/4 cup (150g) granulated sugar
3/4 cup (160g) golden brown sugar, packed
1/2 teaspoon sea salt
1 cup (228g) unsalted butter, cut into 1/4-inch cubes and chilled

Place apple slices in a bowl and toss with lemon juice to prevent apples from oxidizing and turning brown. Add 1/4 cup (50g) sugar and toss to coat. Transfer apples to an airtight container and refrigerate at least 2 hours or overnight.

While apples macerate, make crisp topping: place flour, sugar, brown sugar, and salt in the bowl of a stand mixer fitted with the paddle attachment. Mix on the lowest speed for 1 minute. Gradually add butter on lowest speed until pea-size lumps form, but no longer; the mixture should resemble wet sand. To test, take a handful of the mix—it should hold together for 5 to 10 seconds before crumbling apart. Crisp topping may be used right away or stored in an airtight container in the refrigerator for up to 2 weeks.

Preheat oven to 375°. Lightly coat a 9" x 12" baking dish with nonstick spray. In a small bowl, combine cornstarch, 1/4 cup (50g) sugar, and cinnamon. Set aside. Strain macerated apples. Discard liquid and transfer apples to a large bowl. Add vanilla and cinnamon-sugar mixture. Toss to coat.

Fill baking dish with an even layer of apple slices. Cover apples with crisp topping. Bake on the middle rack until filling looks juicy and topping is pale golden, about 25 minutes. Rotate dish and continue baking until apple filling thickens and bubbles and topping is golden brown and crispy, about 25 more minutes. Let cool 30 minutes before serving.

Tips: It's best to prep the apples a day ahead to allow them to macerate and extract excess liquid. And always taste your fruit to adjust the amount of sugar to the sweetness of the fruit—you want your main ingredient to shine!

BANANA CHOCOLATE BREAD PUDDING WITH SALTY CARAMEL

Stale baguette, overripe banana? Perfect for this pudding. Nothing goes to waste!

Makes one 9" x 13" dish; cut to preferred size

2 French baguettes, cut into $\frac{1}{2}$-inch cubes, toasted, and cooled
12 large eggs
1 $\frac{2}{3}$ cups (333g) granulated sugar
4 $\frac{1}{2}$ cups (1080g) heavy whipping cream
1 $\frac{1}{2}$ cups (352g) whole milk
2 $\frac{1}{4}$ teaspoons vanilla extract
$\frac{3}{4}$ teaspoon sea salt
3 medium ripe bananas, mashed
1 $\frac{1}{2}$ cups (250g) chopped bittersweet chocolate (or chocolate chips)
2 cups Sea Salt Caramel Sauce *(see page 33)*

Place toasted bread in a 4-quart container or bowl and set aside.

In the bowl of a stand mixer fitted with the whisk attachment, whisk eggs on medium speed until broken, about 2 minutes. Decrease speed to low and add sugar. Whisk until smooth. Stream in cream, milk, vanilla extract, and salt and continue to whisk until all ingredients are incorporated, about 1 minute. Pour custard over bread. Let sit for 10 minutes, and then mix by hand to ensure that the bread evenly absorbs the custard. Let sit at least another 10 minutes, or in the refrigerator overnight.

Preheat oven to 350°. Lightly coat a 9" x 13" baking dish with nonstick spray. Transfer bread pudding mixture to pan and spread into an even 1-inch-thick layer. Spread mashed bananas across the bread pudding mixture. Sprinkle half the bittersweet chocolate over the bananas. Spread the remaining bread pudding mixture across the top evenly. Sprinkle the remaining chocolate on top. Cover dish with foil.

Bake 40 minutes, rotate the dish, and continue to bake until custard has set, checking every 10 minutes. Once custard has thickened and set, remove foil and increase oven temperature to 375°. Continue to bake until top is golden brown and crunchy, about 15 minutes. Remove from oven and pour salty caramel sauce on top. Let cool 20 minutes before serving.

STRAWBERRY ALMOND TARTS

During strawberry season we just can't get enough of these beautiful hand-shaped tarts. The jammy runoff from the sheet pan is my favorite sneak treat.

Makes 12 4-inch tarts

All-purpose flour, for dusting
1 recipe (2 disks) Brisée Dough (*see page 22*)
1 recipe Almond Cream (*see recipe below*)
4 cups (660g) strawberries, hulled and quartered
1 egg, for wash
1 tablespoon water
1/2 cup (100g) granulated sugar, for sprinkling
1/4 cup (22g) sliced almonds, toasted

Lightly dust work surface with flour. Roll 1 dough disk out to 3/8-inch thickness. Use a paring knife to cut into 6 5-inch circles. If dough does not yield 6 circles, take the scraps and re-roll to 3/8-inch thickness, then cut remaining circles. Repeat with other dough disk.

Spread 1/2 tablespoon almond cream in the center of each dough circle, leaving a 1/2-inch dough border. Arrange strawberries on top of almond cream. Fold edges up and over filling. Transfer tarts to 2 parchment-lined half-sheet pans, spacing evenly. Chill in the refrigerator 30 minutes.

Preheat oven to 350°. In a small bowl, whisk 1 egg with 1 tablespoon water. Use a pastry brush to apply egg wash to tart edges and generously sprinkle with sugar. Bake, rotating halfway through, until edges of tarts are golden brown and strawberries are jammy, about 30 minutes. Cool, garnish with toasted almonds, and serve.

Almond Cream

1/2 cup (114g) unsalted butter, softened
1/2 cup (100g) granulated sugar
1 cup (114g) finely ground sliced almonds
1 large egg, room temperature
1/8 teaspoon sea salt

In the bowl of a stand mixer fitted with the paddle attachment, cream butter and sugar on medium-low speed until mixture is pale and fluffy, 2 to 3 minutes.

Add almonds and continue to mix for 2 minutes. Scrape bowl well with a rubber spatula to prevent lumps. Add egg and mix until incorporated. Scrape bowl well. Add salt and continue to mix on medium speed until almond cream is fluffy and aerated, about 5 minutes. Store in an airtight container and refrigerate until ready to use. If aerated properly, almond cream should be spreadable when chilled.

Tips: Feel free to change the fruit according to the season—the brisée dough and almond cream are fantastic bases for any fruit. We use strawberries in the spring, peaches in the summer, Concord grapes in the fall, and blood oranges in the winter. The brisée dough and almond cream can be made a day or two ahead.

ALMOND TART

Lindsey Shere and her *Chez Panisse Desserts* taught me about seasonal pastry. Her almond tart is my favorite dessert. I served it at my fiftieth birthday party with brown butter ice cream.

Makes one 8½-inch tart

Sucrée Dough
1 cup (120g) all-purpose flour
1 tablespoon granulated sugar
½ cup (114g) unsalted butter, cut into ½-inch cubes
    and chilled
1 tablespoon ice cold water
½ teaspoon vanilla extract

Filling
1 cup (240g) heavy whipping cream
1 cup (200g) granulated sugar
¼ teaspoon wildflower honey
⅛ teaspoon sea salt
1⅔ cups (144g) sliced almonds
¼ teaspoon almond extract
½ teaspoon orange zest

In the bowl of a stand mixer fitted with the paddle attachment, combine flour and sugar on low speed for 30 seconds. Add cold butter and mix on the lowest speed until pea-size lumps form, about 5 minutes. Add cold water and vanilla extract and mix on the lowest speed until dough comes together and is smooth, about 3 minutes. Remove dough from bowl and shape into a ½-inch-thick disk. Cover with plastic wrap and chill in the refrigerator until firm, about 30 minutes (more is fine).

Preheat oven to 375°. Lightly coat an 8½-inch fluted tart pan (with removable bottom) with nonstick spray and set aside. Remove chilled dough from refrigerator and sandwich between two sheets of plastic wrap. Roll into a 10-inch circle. If dough is very cold and firm, use the palms of your hands to warm the dough until pliable. Remove plastic wrap and gently lay the dough into the tart pan as if tucking in a blanket. Press the dough down, especially along the corners and edges of the tart pan, to prevent air pockets and to yield straight, fluted edges. Trim excess dough from the edge of the tart pan. Chill in the freezer for 15 minutes.

Remove tart from freezer and lightly coat with nonstick spray. Line tart with parchment paper and pie weights or beans and bake until sides are golden, about 20 minutes. Remove parchment paper and pie weights and bake until tart bottom is golden, about 10 more minutes. (The process of baking a crust before adding the filling is known as blind baking.) Remove tart from oven and set aside to cool.

Place cream, sugar, honey, and salt in a medium saucepan over medium heat. Allow mixture to boil and foam, then continue cooking until light golden, 8 to 10 minutes. Remove from heat and stir in almonds, almond extract, and orange zest. Scrape filling into the blind-baked tart shell.

Bake until almond filling bubbles and has caramelized to golden brown, about 30 minutes. Rotate pan and continue baking, checking every 5 minutes, until tart has caramelized to a deeper golden brown around the edges with a blond spot in the center, at least 15 more minutes. Lindsey Shere describes the desired coloring as like "a coffee with a touch of cream in it." Baking may take up to 1 hour total. Remove from oven and let cool for at least 30 minutes before unmolding. Let cool for another 2 hours before serving.

LEMON MERINGUE PIE

Stack it high and watch it fly!

Makes one 10-inch pie

1/2 recipe (about 500g) Brisée Dough (*see page 22*)
1 cup + 2 tablespoons (225g) granulated sugar + another 1 1/2 cups (300g)
5 tablespoons cornstarch
1/4 teaspoon sea salt
1 cup (235g) whole milk, divided
1/2 cup (111g) water
6 large eggs, separated
1/2 cup + 2 tablespoons (150g) fresh lemon juice
2 tablespoons lemon zest
2 teaspoons butter, cut into 1/4-inch cubes and chilled

Lightly coat a 10-inch pie pan with nonstick spray and set aside. Take out chilled dough. Lightly flour work surface and roll dough into a 15-inch circle with 1/8-inch thickness. Gently fold in half and then fold in half again, so dough is quartered. Transfer dough to pie pan with the folded corner in the center. Unfold dough, gently laying it into pan. Press dough into bottom of pie pan and tuck into edges and sides of pan to prevent air gaps. Roll dough overhang under itself to create a crust, and flute the edge. Freeze formed pie shell for at least 1 hour.

Preheat oven to 375°. Remove chilled pie shell from freezer. Place pie shell on a sheet pan and line with parchment paper. Fill with pie weights or dried beans. Blind bake until crust edges are golden and opaque, 25 to 30 minutes. Remove parchment and pie weights and continue to bake until bottom of pie shell is opaque and light golden brown, 10 to 15 minutes. Decrease oven temperature to 350°.

Combine 1 cup + 2 tablespoons (225g) sugar, cornstarch, and salt in a medium saucepan. Whisk in 3/4 (177g) cup milk and water and set over medium heat. Stir constantly with a heat-resistant rubber spatula until mixture thickens to *nappé*, or coats the back of the spoon, about 8 minutes.

In a medium bowl, whisk together egg yolks and 1/4 (58g) cup milk. Pour about 1/4 cup of the cornstarch mixture into the yolk mixture and whisk together to temper. Gradually pour in the remaining cornstarch mixture and whisk until fully incorporated.

Return mixture to saucepan. Add lemon juice and zest. Whisk over medium heat until mixture simmers. Whisk in butter and remove from heat. Mixture will have thickened. Pour lemon custard into blind-baked pie shell. Bake until custard sets, about 15 minutes. It should wobble but not wave. Let cool.

Pour 1 1/2 (300g) cups sugar in an even layer on a parchment-lined sheet pan. Place in oven to heat for 8 minutes. Meanwhile, place egg whites in the clean, dry bowl of a stand mixer fitted with the whip attachment. Whisk on medium speed until frothy. Remove heated sugar from oven and add to egg whites, carefully picking up the two sides of parchment paper to pour. Whisk egg whites and sugar together on high speed until meringue is medium-stiff, about 15 minutes. Meringue will look shiny and glossy. Decrease speed to medium-low to stabilize meringue for 1 minute. Use a rubber spatula to arrange meringue on top of the lemon custard.

Increase oven temperature to 400° and bake until meringue peaks brown, about 8 minutes. Alternatively, use a torch to toast meringue.

PLUM BOURBON CRUMBLE PIE

Anything crumble has my full attention. I always loved Entenmann's crumble coffee cake when I was growing up. Dress it up with a good shake of powdered sugar.

Makes one 10-inch pie

1/2 recipe (about 500g) Brisée Dough (*see page 22*)
1/2 cup (100g) granulated sugar
1 vanilla bean, split lengthwise and seeded
2 tablespoons cornstarch
6 cups (990g) Santa Rosa or other dark-skinned plums, sliced 1/4 inch thick
2 tablespoons bourbon
3 cups Crisp Topping (see *page 32*)

Lightly coat a 10-inch pie pan with nonstick spray and set aside. Take out chilled dough. Lightly flour work surface and roll dough out into a 15-inch circle with 1/8-inch thickness. Gently fold in half and then fold in half again, so dough is quartered. Transfer dough to pie pan with the folded corner in the center. Unfold dough, gently laying it into pan. Press dough into bottom of pie pan and tuck into edges and sides of pan to prevent air gaps. Roll dough overhang under itself to create a crust, and flute the edge. Freeze formed pie shell for at least 1 hour.

Place sugar and vanilla bean and seeds in a large bowl. Rub sugar on the vanilla bean to remove all the seeds. Add cornstarch and mix until combined. Add plums and bourbon and toss to coat. Set aside to macerate for 30 minutes.

Preheat oven to 375°. Remove pie shell from freezer and place on a sheet pan. Line shell with parchment paper and fill with pie weights or dried beans. Bake until crust is golden and opaque, 25 to 30 minutes. Remove parchment paper and pie weights and continue to bake uncovered until bottom of pie shell is opaque and light golden brown, 10 to 15 minutes.

Remove vanilla bean and fill blind-baked shell with plum mixture. Cover with crisp topping. Bake, rotating halfway through, until plum mixture bubbles, juices thicken into a jam, and topping is golden brown, about 1 hour. Let cool 2 hours before serving.

Chov crinkle

almonds mix cross snowball

COOKIES

So many cookies. So little time. Everyone has their favorite cookies, usually based on childhood memories. Mine were Nutter Butters and Pecan Sandies. Our customers all have their special ones, too. They'll stand at the counter and pick out which cookie in a stack is speaking to them. Recreating those old standards is fun! Cecilia and I have made thousands and thousands of cookies over the years. Here are our favorites.

SALTED CHOCOLATE BOUCHONS

Whenever I see these little pastries in the case at Little Flower, I think of perfect little soldiers standing at attention, waiting to be eaten. They are dense, chocolaty, salty, and irresistible.

Makes 20

1/2 cup (100g) granulated sugar
1 cup (213g) golden brown sugar, packed
1 1/2 cups (135g) Dutch-processed cocoa powder
1 tablespoon ground espresso
1/2 teaspoon sea salt
3/4 cup (171g) unsalted butter, melted and kept warm
2 tablespoons extra-virgin olive oil
3 large eggs
3/4 cup (90g) all-purpose flour, sifted
2 tablespoons Maldon sea salt, for sprinkling

Preheat oven to 375°. Lightly coat bouchon molds with nonstick spray and set aside on a sheet pan.

In the bowl of a stand mixer fitted with the paddle attachment, combine sugar, brown sugar, cocoa powder, ground espresso, and salt on low speed for 30 seconds. Stream in melted butter and olive oil on low speed. Mix until combined, about 3 minutes. Scrape bowl well.

Add eggs one at a time on low speed. Scrape bowl well after each addition. Add flour on low speed and mix until just incorporated, about 15 seconds. Scrape bowl well.

Scoop batter into bouchon molds and level with a small offset spatula. Bake until batter has risen and formed small cracks, about 10 minutes. Rotate pan and continue baking until a toothpick comes out clean, about 8 more minutes. Let cool 5 minutes before unmolding. Sprinkle with salt.

Tip: If you don't have bouchon molds, mini cupcake tins will work.

COCONUT MACAROONS

A classic, must-have recipe. Tender, crunchy, and not too sweet.

Makes 18

5 extra-large (3/4 cup + 2 tablespoons or 165g) egg whites
1 3/4 cups (350g) granulated sugar
1 1/2 teaspoons vanilla extract
6 cups (510g) sweetened shredded coconut
1 cup (120g) all-purpose flour

Fill a medium saucepan one third with water and place over medium heat. Bring to a simmer. This is the base for your bain marie, or double boiler. Use a bowl that will nestle on top of the saucepan without touching the simmering water. Whisk egg whites and sugar together in the mixing bowl and set it on top of the simmering water. Continue to whisk mixture vigorously until sugar has dissolved, 5 to 8 minutes. Check by rubbing the liquid between your fingers—if there's graininess, continue whisking.

Pour mixture into the bowl of a stand mixer fitted with the paddle attachment. Add vanilla, coconut, and flour and mix on low speed until well incorporated, about 30 seconds. Scrape bowl well and finish mixing by hand with a rubber spatula.

Lightly coat a parchment-lined sheet pan with nonstick spray. Shape dough into 2-inch balls by hand, or with a #20 yellow scoop, and set onto prepared pan. Tuck any stray strands of coconut under the formed ball. Freeze overnight or until firm, at least 1 hour. Frozen cookie dough will keep in airtight container in the freezer for up to 2 weeks.

Preheat oven to 375°. Set cookies 1/2 inch apart on parchment-lined sheet pan. Bake, rotating halfway through, until crust is golden brown and crispy, about 16 minutes.

CHOCOLATE PEPPERMINT SNOWBALLS

Hello holidays! There's nothing quite like peppermint to get you in the holiday mood.

Makes 15

1 cup (228g) Brown Butter (*see page 32*), softened, but not liquid
2 cups + 1 tablespoon (258g) powdered sugar, divided
1 teaspoon vanilla extract
1 1/2 teaspoons peppermint flavoring
2 1/2 cups + 1 tablespoon (310g) all-purpose flour
3/4 teaspoon sea salt
3/4 cup (175g) mini chocolate chips

In the bowl of a stand mixer fitted with the paddle attachment, combine brown butter and 1 cup plus 1 tablespoon (133g) powdered sugar on medium-low speed for 30 seconds. Use a rubber spatula to scrape bowl. Add vanilla extract and peppermint flavoring and mix on low speed for 30 seconds. Scrape bowl well.

Add flour and salt and mix on low speed until just incorporated, about 20 seconds. Add mini chocolate chips and mix on low speed very briefly until just combined, about 10 seconds. Scrape bowl well and finish incorporating dry ingredients with a rubber spatula.

Form dough into 2-inch balls by hand, or with a #20 yellow scoop, and set on a parchment-lined sheet pan. Freeze until firm, at least 1 hour. Frozen cookie dough will keep in an airtight container for up to 2 weeks.

Preheat oven to 375°. Place cookies 1 inch apart on parchment-lined sheet pan. Bake until dough is slightly puffed, about 8 minutes. Rotate pan and continue baking until edges are golden and small cracks appear, about 7 more minutes. Let cool for 5 minutes, and then coat warm cookies with remaining 1 cup (125g) powdered sugar.

FLORENTINES

Even though I couldn't afford to actually buy them, I used to go visit these dreamy disks of fruit, nuts, and caramel at Le Bon Marché in Paris.

Gluten-free

Makes 12

1/4 cup + 1 tablespoon (73g) whole milk
1/2 cup (100g) granulated sugar
2 tablespoons + 1 1/2 teaspoons (45g) wildflower honey
1/2 cup (114g) unsalted butter, softened
1/4 teaspoon vanilla extract
1/8 teaspoon sea salt
1 1/2 cups (130g) sliced almonds
1/4 cup (27g) pepitas
1/4 cup (35g) sunflower seeds
Zest of 1/2 medium orange

Preheat oven to 350°. Lightly coat 2 large 6-mold muffin tins with nonstick spray and set aside. Have a candy thermometer handy.

Combine milk, sugar, and honey in a medium saucepan over medium heat. When mixture reaches 248°, remove from heat.

Use a heat-resistant rubber spatula to stir in butter, vanilla, and salt. Mix until incorporated. Add almonds, pepitas, sunflower seeds, and orange zest and mix until incorporated.

Scoop 2 1/2 tablespoons batter (or use a #24 red scoop) into each muffin mold. Bake 15 minutes. Rotate pan and continue baking until florentines are golden brown and bubbling, about 10 more minutes. Set aside to cool until set, about 5 minutes. Go around the edges of each cookie with a small offset spatula to loosen before removing from molds.

CHOCOLATE CRINKLES

Like beautiful chocolate cookies dipped in snow.

Makes 18

3/4 cup (120g) chopped unsweetened chocolate
1 cup + 1 tablespoon (190g) chopped bittersweet chocolate, 70% cacao
1/4 cup (114g) unsalted butter, softened
4 large eggs
2 1/4 cups (450g) granulated sugar
1 tablespoon vanilla extract
1 tablespoon ground espresso
1 3/4 cups + 2 tablespoons (225g) all-purpose flour, sifted
1/2 cup (45g) Dutch-processed cocoa powder, sifted
1/2 teaspoon sea salt
2 teaspoons baking powder
1 cup (125g) powdered sugar, to coat

Fill a medium saucepan one third with water and place over medium heat. Choose a mixing bowl that will rest nestled on top of saucepan. This will be the bain marie, or double boiler. Combine unsweetened chocolate, bittersweet chocolate, and butter in the bowl, stirring occasionally with a rubber spatula to ensure even melting and to prevent chocolate from burning. When fully melted, remove from heat and set aside.

In the bowl of a stand mixer fitted with the whisk attachment, whisk eggs on medium speed for 30 seconds. Rain in sugar and continue to whisk on medium speed for 1 minute. Increase speed to medium-high and whisk until mixture is thick and pale, about 4 minutes. This is the ribbon stage.

Add vanilla extract and ground espresso and mix on low speed for 15 seconds. Scrape bowl well with rubber spatula. Add melted chocolate mixture and mix on medium-low speed for 30 seconds. Scrape bowl well.

Add flour, cocoa powder, salt, and baking powder and mix on low speed until just incorporated, about 20 seconds. Scrape bowl well.

Pour into a container and chill until firm, about 30 minutes.

Scoop dough into 2-inch balls by hand, or with a #24 red scoop, and set on a parchment-lined sheet pan. Freeze until firm, at least 1 hour. Frozen cookie dough will keep in an airtight container in the freezer for up to 2 weeks.

Preheat oven to 375°. Coat cookies in powdered sugar and set 1 inch apart on a parchment-lined sheet pan. Bake until dough is slightly puffed, about 8 minutes. Rotate pan and continue baking until cookies are puffed up and small crinkles appear, about 7 more minutes.

GINGER MOLASSES COOKIES

This chewy cookie has a spicy flavor that's even better when dunked in icy cold milk.

Makes 18

3/4 cup (171g) Brown Butter (*see page 32*), softened
1 1/2 cups (300g) granulated sugar, divided
1 large egg
1/4 cup (85g) molasses
1 2/3 cups (200g) all-purpose flour, sifted
2 teaspoons baking soda, sifted
1/4 teaspoon sea salt
1 teaspoon ground cinnamon
1/2 teaspoon ground cloves
2 teaspoons grated fresh ginger
1 tablespoon finely chopped candied ginger

In the bowl of a stand mixer fitted with the paddle attachment, cream brown butter and 1 cup (200g) granulated sugar on medium-low speed until smooth. Add egg and mix on low speed until combined. Scrape bowl well. Add molasses and mix on low speed until well combined. Scrape bowl. Add flour, baking soda, salt, cinnamon, cloves, and fresh ginger on low speed until just incorporated. Remove bowl from stand mixer and use a rubber spatula to fold in candied ginger.

Form dough into 2-inch balls by hand, or with a #20 yellow scoop, and place onto a parchment-lined sheet pan. Place remaining 1/2 cup (100g) sugar in a shallow bowl. Coat each dough ball in sugar and return to sheet pan. Gently press cookies flat with your palm so they look like hockey pucks. Freeze overnight or until firm, at least 1 hour. Frozen cookie dough will keep in an airtight container for up to 2 weeks.

Preheat oven to 375°. Place cookies 2 inches apart on a parchment-lined sheet pan. Bake until dough has puffed, about 8 minutes. Rotate and continue baking until edges are golden brown and crispy and cookies look cracked with a soft, chewy center, about 7 more minutes.

CHAI SUGAR COOKIES

A blend of aromatic spices makes this magical cookie extra special.

Makes 12

2 cups (400g) granulated sugar, divided
¼ cup (57g) cream cheese, softened
½ teaspoon ground cinnamon
½ teaspoon ground ginger
½ teaspoon ground cardamom
½ teaspoon ground cloves
6 tablespoons (86g) unsalted butter, melted, warm
⅓ cup (66g) grapeseed oil
1 large egg, room temperature
1 tablespoon whole milk
1 teaspoon vanilla extract
2 ½ cups + 2 tablespoons (320g) all-purpose flour, sifted
1 teaspoon baking powder
½ teaspoon baking soda
½ teaspoon sea salt

In the bowl of a stand mixer fitted with the paddle attachment, cream 1½ cups (300g) sugar, cream cheese, and spices on medium-low speed for 1 minute. Scrape bowl with rubber spatula. Stream in warm butter and mix on low speed for 30 seconds. Stream in oil and mix on low speed for 30 seconds. Add egg, milk, and vanilla and mix until combined. Scrape bowl well. Sift together flour, baking powder, baking soda, and salt and add to the mixing bowl, mixing very briefly on low speed until just incorporated, about 30 seconds. Scrape bowl well and finish incorporating dry ingredients with rubber spatula.

Shape dough into 2-inch balls by hand, or with a #20 yellow scoop, and set on parchment-lined sheet pan. Pour remaining ½ cup (100g) sugar into a shallow bowl and dip each cookie to coat. Space cookies 1 inch apart on pan and gently flatten with your palm so cookies look like hockey pucks. Freeze until firm, at least 1 hour. Frozen cookie dough will keep in an airtight container for up to 2 weeks.

Preheat oven to 375°. Bake until slightly puffed, about 8 minutes. Rotate pan and continue baking until edges are golden and center is pale but not translucent, about 7 more minutes. Finished cookies will look cracked and be soft and chewy in the center.

WHITE CHOCOLATE CHAI COOKIES

Creamy, white, and spicy.

Makes 18

1 cup (228g) unsalted butter, softened
1 cup (213g) golden brown sugar, packed
1 cup (200g) granulated sugar
2 large eggs
1½ teaspoons vanilla extract
3½ cups + 2 tablespoons (438g) all-purpose flour, sifted
1½ teaspoons baking soda
½ teaspoon sea salt
1 teaspoon ground cardamom
½ teaspoon ground cinnamon
½ teaspoon ground ginger
¼ teaspoon ground allspice
2 cups (340g) chopped white chocolate

In the bowl of a stand mixer fitted with the paddle attachment, cream butter and sugars on medium speed until fluffy. Scrape bowl well with a rubber spatula. Add eggs one at a time, mixing until combined and scraping bowl after each addition. Add vanilla extract and mix until combined.

Add flour, baking soda, salt, and spices and mix on low speed until just incorporated. Dough should be a bit dry and shaggy. Scrape bowl well. Fold in chopped white chocolate with a rubber spatula.

Form dough into 2-inch balls by hand, or with a #20 yellow scoop, and set on a parchment-lined sheet pan. Gently press flat with your palm so they look like hockey pucks. Freeze overnight or until firm, at least 1 hour.

Preheat oven to 375°. Bake, rotating halfway through, until edges are golden brown and center is pale, about 15 minutes.

OATMEAL RAISIN COOKIES

My dad's favorite.

Makes 24

1 cup + 3 tablespoons (270g) unsalted butter, softened
1 cup + 1 teaspoon (218g) golden brown sugar, packed
1 1/3 cups (267g) granulated sugar
2 large eggs
3/4 teaspoon vanilla extract
3 tablespoons honey
2 1/4 cups + 3 tablespoons (293g) cake flour, sifted
1/3 cup (40g) all-purpose flour, sifted
1 1/2 teaspoons baking powder
1 teaspoon baking soda
3/4 teaspoon sea salt
1 cup (150g) dark raisins
1 cup (150g) golden raisins
1 1/3 cups (190g) walnuts, chopped
2 3/4 cups + 1 tablespoon (280g) old-fashioned rolled oats

In the bowl of a stand mixer fitted with the paddle attachment, cream butter and sugars on low speed for 30 seconds. Scrape bowl well with a rubber spatula.

Add eggs, one at a time, mixing on low speed until well incorporated, about 1 minute each. Add vanilla extract and honey and mix on low speed for 15 seconds. Scrape bowl well.

Add flours, baking powder, baking soda, and salt and mix on low speed until just incorporated, about 30 seconds. Add raisins, walnuts, and oats and mix on low speed for 15 seconds. Use a rubber spatula to finish incorporating raisins, walnuts, and oats into dough. Be sure to mix dough well so that there aren't any butter or flour clumps.

Form dough into 2-inch balls by hand, or with a #20 yellow scoop, and place onto a parchment-lined sheet pan. Gently press flat with your palm so they look like hockey pucks. Freeze at least 1 hour. Frozen cookies may be stored in an airtight container for up to 2 weeks.

Preheat oven to 375°. Place cookies 1 inch apart on parchment-lined sheet pan. Bake, rotating halfway through, until edges are golden brown and center is blond, soft, and chewy, about 16 minutes.

CHOCOLATE CHIP COOKIES

It's great to have this dough in the freezer for an easy, quick bake. Portion it first to make the process even quicker.

Makes 24

1 cup (228g) unsalted butter, softened
1 cup (213g) golden brown sugar, packed
1 cup (200g) granulated sugar
2 large eggs
1½ teaspoons vanilla extract
3½ cups + 2 tablespoons (438g) all-purpose flour, sifted
1¼ teaspoons baking soda
½ teaspoon sea salt
2 cups (510g) mini chocolate chips

In the bowl of a stand mixer fitted with the paddle attachment, cream butter and sugars on low speed for 30 seconds. Scrape bowl well with a rubber spatula.

Add eggs one at a time, and mix each on low speed until well incorporated, about 2 minutes. Add vanilla and mix to combine. Scrape bowl well.

Add flour, baking soda, and salt on low speed until just incorporated, about 30 seconds. Add mini chocolate chips and mix on low speed for 15 seconds. Use rubber spatula to finish combining chocolate chips into dough.

Shape dough into 2-inch balls by hand or with a #20 yellow scoop. Set cookies at least 1 inch apart on a parchment-lined sheet pan. Gently flatten with your palm so they look like hockey pucks. Freeze until firm, at least 1 hour. Frozen cookie dough will keep in an airtight container for up to 2 weeks.

Preheat oven to 375°. Bake, rotating halfway through, until edges are golden brown with a blond, soft, and chewy center, about 16 minutes.

CHOCOLATE PEANUT BUTTER COOKIES

Remember the Reese's commercial in which the guy eating the chocolate bar falls into the guy eating the peanut butter? This is just that, only in a cookie.

Makes 48

Crunchy Peanut Butter Cookie Dough

1 cup (228g) unsalted butter, softened
1 1/2 cups (405g) creamy peanut butter
1 cup (200g) granulated sugar
1 cup (213g) golden brown sugar, packed
2 large eggs
1 teaspoon vanilla extract
2 1/3 cups (280g) all-purpose flour, sifted
1 1/2 teaspoons baking soda
3 cups (470g) salted peanuts, chopped

In the bowl of a stand mixer fitted with the paddle attachment, cream butter, peanut butter, and sugars on low speed for 30 seconds. Scrape bowl well with a rubber spatula. Add eggs one at a time on low speed, scraping bowl after each addition. Add vanilla and mix on low speed for 1 minute. Add flour and baking soda and mix on low speed until just combined, about 15 seconds. Add peanuts and mix on low speed until just incorporated, about 15 seconds. Use a rubber spatula to finish incorporating flour and peanuts by hand. Transfer dough to a large bowl, cover, and set aside.

Chocolate Cookie Dough

1 1/2 cups (342g) unsalted butter, softened
1 1/2 cups (320g) golden brown sugar, packed
1 1/2 cups (300g) granulated sugar
3 large eggs
2 1/4 teaspoons vanilla extract
3 cups (360g) all-purpose flour, sifted
2 1/2 cups + 2 tablespoons (240g) Dutch-processed
    cocoa powder, sifted
1 tablespoon baking soda
1 1/2 teaspoons sea salt

In the bowl of a stand mixer fitted with the paddle attachment, cream butter and sugars on medium speed until fluffy. Scrape bowl well with a rubber spatula. Add eggs one at a time and mix until combined. Scrape bowl well. Add vanilla and mix until combined. Sift together flour, cocoa powder, baking soda, and salt and add to wet ingredients. Mix on low speed until just incorporated. Scrape bowl well.

Assembly

Form each kind of dough into 1-inch balls. Take one ball of each dough and smoosh them together to create one 2-inch ball. Or, using a #20 yellow scoop, fill half the scoop with peanut butter dough and the rest with chocolate dough. Set dough balls onto a sheet pan lined with parchment paper. Gently flatten with your palm so they look like hockey pucks. Freeze overnight or until firm, at least 1 hour. Frozen cookie dough will keep in an airtight container for up to 2 weeks.

   Preheat oven to 375°. Set cookies on parchment-lined sheet pans, spaced 1 inch apart. Bake, rotating halfway through, until edges are golden brown, about 16 minutes.

PEANUT BUTTER COOKIES

Smooth or crunchy? I'm a crunchy person, but we use smooth in the bakery to make this delicious cookie. For a fun variation, add some chopped salted peanuts to the tops before baking.

Makes 12

1 cup (228g) unsalted butter, softened
1 1/2 cups (405g) creamy peanut butter
1 cup (200g) granulated sugar
1 cup (213g) golden brown sugar, packed
2 large eggs
1 teaspoon vanilla extract
2 1/3 cups (280g) all-purpose flour, sifted
1 1/2 teaspoons baking soda
1/2 cup (111g) boiling water

In the bowl of a stand mixer fitted with the paddle attachment, cream butter, peanut butter, and sugars on low speed for 30 seconds. Scrape bowl well with a rubber spatula. Add eggs one at a time on low speed, scraping bowl after each addition. Add vanilla extract and mix on low speed for 1 minute. Add flour and baking soda and mix on low speed until just combined, about 15 seconds. Use rubber spatula to finish incorporating by hand.

Form dough into 2-inch balls by hand, or with a #20 yellow scoop, and set on a parchment-lined sheet pan. Gently press cookies flat with your palm so they look like hockey pucks. Chill in freezer for 15 minutes.

Set a fork in a small bowl of boiling water. Remove cookies from freezer and use warm fork to mark cookies with a crisscross pattern. Return dough to freezer and chill for at least 1 hour.

Preheat oven to 375°. Set cookies 1 inch apart on a parchment-lined sheet pan. Bake, rotating halfway through, until edges are golden brown, about 15 minutes.

GLUTEN-FREE PEANUT BUTTER COOKIES

Crispy, chewy, simple, and delicious!
Gluten-free

Makes 16

2 cups (540g) creamy peanut butter
1 cup (213g) golden brown sugar, packed
1 cup (200g) granulated sugar
2 large eggs
2 tablespoons vanilla extract
2 teaspoons baking soda
1 tablespoon Maldon sea salt, for sprinkling

In the bowl of a stand mixer fitted with the paddle attachment, cream peanut butter and sugars on low speed until combined, about 1 minute. Scrape bowl well with rubber spatula. Add eggs one at a time, mixing until combined. Scrape bowl well. Add vanilla and baking soda and mix on low speed until combined.

Form dough into 2-inch balls by hand, or with a #20 yellow scoop, and place onto a parchment-lined sheet pan. Gently press cookies flat with your palm so they look like hockey pucks. Freeze overnight or until firm, at least 1 hour. Frozen cookie dough will keep in an airtight container for up to 2 weeks.

Preheat oven to 375°. Place cookies onto parchment-lined sheet pan, spaced 1 1/2 inches apart. Sprinkle with salt. Bake, rotating halfway through, until cookies spread and crack, about 15 minutes.

CHOCOLATE SEA SALT CARAMEL COOKIES

Salty and chewy, this cookie is one of my very favorites. Use good-quality cocoa powder for a dark-chocolate flavor, and you'll be in heaven.

Makes 18

1 cup (228g) unsalted butter, softened

1 cup (213g) golden brown sugar, packed

1 cup (200g) granulated sugar

2 large eggs

1 1/2 teaspoons vanilla extract

2 cups (240g) all-purpose flour, sifted

1 3/4 cups (160g) Dutch-processed cocoa powder, sifted

2 teaspoons baking soda

1 teaspoon sea salt

18 sea salt caramels, cut into 1/2-inch cubes

2 tablespoons Maldon sea salt, for sprinkling

In the bowl of a stand mixer fitted with the paddle attachment, cream butter and sugars on medium speed until fluffy. Scrape bowl well with a rubber spatula. Add eggs one at a time, mixing on low speed until combined. Scrape bowl well. Add vanilla extract. Sift together flour, cocoa powder, baking soda, and salt and add to wet mixture. Mix on low speed until just incorporated. Scrape bowl well.

Shape dough into 2-inch balls by hand, or with a #20 yellow scoop, and set them onto a parchment-lined sheet pan. Gently flatten with your palm so they look like hockey pucks. Place a sea salt caramel in the center of each cookie. Freeze overnight or until firm, at least 1 hour. Frozen cookie dough will keep in an airtight container in the freezer for up to 2 weeks.

Preheat oven to 375°. Bake, rotating halfway through, until caramel center bubbles and spreads, about 15 minutes. Remove from oven, sprinkle sea salt onto each cookie, and cool on a rack.

BROWN BUTTER SHORTBREAD

My favorite cookie. There: I said it. Now try it and see if you agree.

Makes 18

1 cup (228g) unsalted Brown Butter (*see page 32*), cooled
1/2 cup + 2 tablespoons (133g) golden brown sugar, packed
1 tablespoon vanilla extract
1 1/2 teaspoons sea salt
2 1/3 cups (280g) all-purpose flour, sifted
1/4 cup (55g) turbinado sugar

In the bowl of a stand mixer fitted with the paddle attachment, combine brown butter, brown sugar, vanilla, and salt on low speed for 30 seconds. Scrape bowl well with a rubber spatula.

Add flour and mix on low speed until just combined, about 15 seconds. Use rubber spatula to incorporate flour mixture by hand. Dough should feel like wet sand–tacky but not sticky or greasy.

Transfer dough onto a parchment-lined sheet pan and gently pat it into a 1/2-inch-thick rectangle. Let stand for at least 2 hours, preferably overnight. Do not refrigerate.

Cut dough with a 1 1/2-inch-round cutter. Pat any scraps back together at a 1/2-inch thickness to form more cookies. Transfer cookies to a parchment-lined sheet pan and freeze overnight.

Preheat oven to 375°. Lightly coat 12-mold muffin tins with nonstick spray. Place one cookie into each muffin mold. Bake, rotating halfway through, until edges are golden brown, about 15 minutes. Sprinkle cookies with turbinado sugar and continue baking 2 more minutes. Cool 10 minutes before unmolding.

Tip: Make brown butter a day ahead, to allow it to cool and set before starting on cookies. Brown butter is a delicious staple to have on hand in the refrigerator. It makes a great addition to vegetables, fish, rice, pasta... the possibilities are endless.

PINK PEPPERCORN HIBISCUS SHORTBREAD

A real departure from Scottish shortbread, this one is spiced with pink peppercorns and hibiscus sugar. It's just beautiful.

Makes 12 wedges

1/4 cup + 2 tablespoons (47g) powdered sugar

1/4 cup + 1 teaspoon (54g) granulated sugar

1 teaspoon sea salt

1 1/4 cups (150g) cake flour

1 1/4 cups (150g) all-purpose flour

1 tablespoon white rice flour

1 teaspoon pink peppercorns, coarsely ground

1 cup (228g) European-style butter (at least 82% butterfat), such as Plugra, cut into 1/4-inch cubes and chilled

1/2 teaspoon ground dried hibiscus

1 tablespoon sanding or decorative sugar

Preheat oven to 375°. Line a shallow 9-inch-round cake pan with parchment paper and lightly coat with nonstick spray. Set aside.

Place sugars, salt, flours, and peppercorns into a food processor. Blend together for 30 seconds. Add cold butter a few pieces at a time, pulsing after each addition. Continue to blend until butter is fully incorporated and dough pulls away from sides of processor.

Press dough into cake pan. Bake 25 minutes. Rotate pan and continue baking until top and edges are golden brown, about 15 more minutes.

Combine ground hibiscus and sanding sugar in small bowl. Sprinkle hibiscus sugar on shortbread and bake 5 more minutes. Let cool 15 minutes before unmolding. Use a chef's knife to cut into 12 wedges.

Tip: Dried hibiscus is sold by most tea merchants, and you can also find it online .

THYME SHORTBREAD

Savory herbs are so good with a little butter and sugar! We especially love thyme: tiny leaves of flavor.

Makes 30

1 cup (228g) European-style butter (at least 82% butterfat), such as Plugra, softened
3/4 cup (150g) granulated sugar
1 large egg
1 teaspoon vanilla extract
2 2/3 cups (320g) all-purpose flour, sifted
1 tablespoon white rice flour, sifted
1 1/2 teaspoons sea salt
1 tablespoon fresh thyme, chopped
1/2 cup (110g) sanding or decorative sugar

In the bowl of a stand mixer fitted with the paddle attachment, cream butter and sugar on medium-low speed until fluffy and pale yellow. Scrape bowl well. Add egg and vanilla. Mix on low speed until incorporated. Scrape bowl well. Add dry ingredients on low speed until just incorporated, about 30 seconds. Set a sheet of parchment paper on flat work surface. Scrape bowl and transfer dough to parchment paper. Roll dough into a log with a 2-inch diameter. Wrap in parchment and chill in refrigerator until firm, at least 1 hour.

Preheat oven to 375°. Remove chilled dough from refrigerator, unwrap, and leave log in center of parchment paper. Pour sanding sugar next to log and roll log to coat all sides. Use a chef's knife to slice into 1/4- to 3/8-inch-thick cookies. Place cookies on parchment-lined sheet pan with 1/2-inch spacing. Bake, rotating halfway through, until edges of cookies are golden brown, about 15 minutes. Cool and serve.

Sablés, top; Thyme Shortbread, bottom

SABLÉS

The perfect little cookie, the sablé is sandy and buttery, not too sweet, and so satisfying. Try the lavender variation—it will take you to the south of France.

Makes 20

2 1/4 cups (270g) all-purpose flour, plus more for dusting
1/2 cup (62g) powdered sugar
2 1/2 tablespoons granulated sugar
1/4 teaspoon sea salt
1 cup (228g) European-style butter (at least 82% butterfat), such as Plugra, cut into 1/4-inch cubes and chilled
2 teaspoons vanilla extract
Royal Icing (*see page 61*), optional

In the bowl of a stand mixer fitted with the paddle attachment, combine flour, sugars, and salt on low speed for 30 seconds. Gradually add butter and paddle until mixture is coarse and crumbly, about 2 minutes. Add vanilla and continue to mix on low speed until dough comes together and butter is fully incorporated, 5 to 8 minutes.

Pat dough into 1/2-inch-thick rectangle. Wrap with plastic film and chill until firm, about 1 hour. Dough may be stored in the refrigerator for up to 1 week.

Lightly dust work surface with flour and roll dough 1/4 inch thick. Dip a 3-inch fluted round or other shape cutter into a small, shallow bowl of flour to cut dough. Transfer cut sablés to a parchment-lined sheet pan. Freeze until firm, at least 20 minutes.

Preheat oven to 375°. Place cookies 1/2 inch apart on parchment-lined sheet pan. Bake, rotating halfway through, until edges turn golden brown, about 16 minutes. Decorate with Royal Icing, if you like.

Variations

Matcha: Substitute 1 tablespoon plus 1 teaspoon matcha powder for an equal amount of the flour.

Chocolate: Substitute 2 tablespoons plus 2 teaspoons (20g) white rice flour and 1/3 cup (40g) Dutch-processed cocoa powder for 1/2 cup (60g) of the all-purpose flour.

Lavender: Add 2 tablespoons dried lavender buds to the flour mixture. Roll dough out as above, but use a chef's knife to cut into 3-inch squares instead of circles. Continue as with the main recipe.

BUCKWHEAT SABLÉS

Inspired by our friend Sonoko Sakai of Common Grains, Cecilia developed this cookie for Roxana Jullapat and her fundraiser for the Edible Schoolyard in Los Angeles. We love our community of fellow cooks and bakers.

Note: If you don't have white groats, brown will be fine—they're just a little less tender.

Makes 24

3/4 cup + 2 tablespoons (200g) unsalted butter, softened
1/2 cup + 1 tablespoon (113g) granulated sugar
1/2 vanilla bean, split lengthwise and scraped
1 cup (120g) all-purpose flour, plus more for dusting
1 cup (113g) whole-wheat flour
1/2 teaspoon Fleur de Sel de Guérande salt
1/3 cup (58g) organic white buckwheat groats

In the bowl of a stand mixer fitted with paddle attachment, cream butter, sugar, and vanilla bean seeds on low speed for 30 seconds.

Add flours and salt and mix on low speed until just incorporated, about 30 seconds. Add groats and mix on low speed for 15 seconds.

Turn out dough onto a lightly floured surface and form into a 1/2-inch-thick rectangle. Wrap with plastic wrap and chill until firm, about 1 hour. Dough will keep in the refrigerator up to 1 week.

Lightly dust work surface with flour. Roll dough 1/4 inch thick. Dip a 3-inch-round cutter into a small, shallow bowl of all-purpose flour to cut dough. Transfer cookies to a parchment-lined sheet pan. Freeze until firm, at least 20 minutes.

Preheat oven to 375°. Arrange cookies evenly on parchment-lined sheet pan at least 1/2 inch apart. Bake, rotating halfway through, until edges are golden brown, about 16 minutes.

SALTED SABLÉS BRETONS

A lovely little treat. Try the lime variation—it's like a margarita in a cookie!

Makes 24

2/3 cup (150g) Echire salted butter, softened

2 teaspoons sea salt

4 egg yolks

1 cup (200g) granulated sugar

1 3/4 cups (210g) all-purpose flour, sifted, plus more for dusting

2 tablespoons baking powder

1 egg, for wash

In the bowl of a stand mixer fitted with the paddle attachment, cream butter and salt on low speed until smooth, about 30 seconds.

In a medium bowl, whisk egg yolks, slowly adding sugar. Whisk until mixture is light and fluffy, but no longer. Add this yolk mixture to butter mixture, mixing on low speed until well incorporated. Add flour and baking powder on low speed until just incorporated.

Pat dough into a 1/2-inch-thick rectangle. Wrap with plastic film and chill until firm, about 1 hour. Dough may be stored in the refrigerator up to 1 week.

Lightly dust work surface with flour. Roll dough 1/2 inch thick. Dip a 2-inch-round cutter into a small, shallow bowl of flour to cut dough into cookies. Transfer sablés to a parchment-lined sheet pan, spaced 1/2 inch apart. Freeze until firm, at least 20 minutes.

Preheat oven to 375°. Beat egg in a small bowl and apply egg wash with pastry brush. Use the tines of a fork to etch cross-hatch marks on top of each cookie. Bake, rotating halfway through, until edges are golden brown, about 20 minutes.

Variation: Lime
Add zest of 2 limes and 1/2 teaspoon ground kaffir lime leaves to sugar. Rub zest and ground lime leaves with sugar to release oils and aromatics.

Tip: Butter is the star of this cookie. We recommend salted Échiré; Straus salted and Vermont Creamery salted butter are fantastic substitutes.

MERINGUES

Pillowy piles of meringues always make me think of Paris. We've adapted this recipe from Ottolenghi.

Makes 24

1½ cups (300g) granulated sugar
4 extra-large (¾ cup or 150g) egg whites, room temperature
1 teaspoon vanilla extract
¼ teaspoon sea salt

Preheat oven to 350°. Spread sugar evenly onto parchment-lined sheet pan. Heat sugar in oven until golden, about 5 minutes.

While sugar is baking, place egg whites in the clean, dry bowl of a stand mixer fitted with the whisk attachment. Whip egg whites on medium speed until frothy. When sugar is ready, carefully lift corners of parchment paper together and pour hot sugar into egg whites. Add vanilla extract and salt. Increase speed to high and continue to whip until meringue is medium stiff and glossy.

Lower oven temperature to 200°. Use a tablespoon to dollop meringues onto parchment-lined sheet pan with ½ inch of space between each. Bake until exterior and bottom are dry and firm, about 2 hours. Turn off oven and leave meringues in oven overnight. Store in airtight container for up to 1 week.

Variations
Raspberry Rose: Replace vanilla extract with rosewater and gently fold in 1 tablespoon raspberry jam and ½ teaspoon red food coloring before baking, leaving color streaky.
Orange Blossom: Replace vanilla extract with orange blossom water and gently fold in ½ teaspoon orange food coloring.
Lemon: Gently fold in the zest of 1 lemon and ½ teaspoon yellow food coloring.

PECAN SANDIES

These were always my choice as a kid when I got to choose cookies at the A&P. Cecilia makes perfect ones.

Makes 24

1 cup (228g) Brown Butter (*see page 32*), softened but not liquid
1 cup (125g) powdered sugar, plus 1/2 cup (62g) more for dusting
1 teaspoon vanilla extract
2 1/3 cups (280g) all-purpose flour, sifted, plus more for dusting
3/4 teaspoon sea salt
1 1/2 cups (170g) pecan pieces

In the bowl of a stand mixer fitted with the paddle attachment, cream brown butter and 1 cup (125g) powdered sugar on low speed for 1 minute. Scrape bowl well with a rubber spatula. Add vanilla and mix on low speed for 15 seconds. Scrape bowl well.

Add flour and salt and mix on low speed until just incorporated, about 30 seconds. Scrape bowl well. Add pecan pieces and mix on low speed until just combined, about 15 seconds.

Sandwich dough between two sheets of parchment paper and roll out to a 3/8-inch thickness. Let stand for 2 hours.

Dip a 2 1/2-inch-round cutter into a shallow bowl of flour and cut out cookies. Roll out scraps to 3/8-inch thickness to cut more cookies. Transfer sandies onto a parchment-lined sheet pan and freeze at least 30 minutes. Dough may be stored in an airtight container for up to 2 weeks.

Preheat oven to 375°. Place cookies, spaced 1 inch apart, on parchment-lined sheet pan. Bake, rotating halfway through, until edges are golden brown, about 16 minutes.

BROWNIES

I love our brownie recipe. Not too sweet and not too cakey, it's just perfect: chewy, rich, and delicious.

Makes one 9″ x 13″ dish; cut to preferred size

1 cup (170g) chopped unsweetened chocolate
1 cup (170g) chopped bittersweet chocolate, 70% cacao
1 cup (228g) unsalted butter
5 large eggs
1¼ cups (250g) granulated sugar
1½ cups (320g) golden brown sugar, packed
1 teaspoon vanilla extract
1⅔ cups (200g) all-purpose flour, sifted
1½ teaspoons baking powder
¾ teaspoon sea salt

Preheat oven to 375°. Lightly coat a 9″ x 13″ baking dish with nonstick spray and set aside.

Fill a medium saucepan one third with water and place over medium heat. Choose a mixing bowl that will rest nestled on top of saucepan to make a double boiler. Place chocolates and butter in the bowl, stirring occasionally with a rubber spatula to ensure even melting and to prevent chocolate from burning. When fully melted, remove from heat.

In the bowl of a stand mixer fitted with the whisk attachment, whisk eggs on medium speed for 30 seconds. Decrease speed to low and add sugars. When combined, whisk on medium speed for 1 minute. Increase speed to medium-high and whisk for 4 minutes until mixture is thick and pale. This is the ribbon stage.

Add vanilla and mix on low speed for 15 seconds. Scrape bowl well with rubber spatula. Add melted chocolate mixture on medium-low speed, mixing for 30 seconds. Scrape bowl well.

Add flour, baking powder, and salt all at once and mix on low speed until just incorporated but no longer, about 20 seconds. Scrape bowl well.

Pour batter into prepared pan. Bake until batter has risen and looks like a soufflé, about 30 minutes, rotate pan, and continue baking until a toothpick comes out clean, about 30 more minutes.

FENNEL BLONDIES

I love licorice. This recipe is like adding licorice and butterscotch together. Yum.

Makes one 9″ x 13″ dish; cut to preferred size

2 1/2 cups (570g) unsalted butter
6 large eggs
1 cup (200g) granulated sugar
4 cups (852g) golden brown sugar
1 1/2 tablespoons vanilla extract
4 1/2 cups (540g) all-purpose flour, sifted
1 tablespoon baking powder
1 tablespoon sea salt
1 teaspoon dried fennel seeds, ground
2 cups (180g) diced fresh fennel

Preheat oven to 375°. Lightly coat a 9″ x 13″ baking dish with nonstick spray and set aside.

Place butter in a medium saucepan. Bring to a boil and lower heat to medium. Use a wooden spoon or heat-resistant spatula to stir and scrape any milk solids off bottom of saucepan. The milk solids will continue to brown, yielding the nutty, brown bits of love. Allow butter to foam a second time. Remove from heat and set aside.

In the bowl of a stand mixer fitted with the whisk attachment, whisk eggs on medium speed for 30 seconds. Decrease speed to low and add sugars. Whisk on medium speed for 1 minute. Increase speed to medium-high and whisk for 4 minutes until mixture is thick and pale. This is the ribbon stage.

Add vanilla and mix on low speed for 15 seconds. Scrape bowl well with rubber spatula. Stream in warm brown butter, making sure to scrape all brown bits into batter. Mix on low speed until incorporated, about 1 minute. Scrape bowl well.

Add flour, baking powder, salt, and ground fennel and mix on low speed until just incorporated, about 20 seconds. Scrape bowl well. Fold in fresh fennel.

Pour batter into prepared pan. Bake until batter has risen like a soufflé, about 30 minutes, and then rotate pan and continue baking until toothpick comes out clean, about 30 more minutes.

RASPBERRY FOLEY BARS

Named for my friend Stephanie Foley, this recipe can also work as a delicious cake. The bars are dense and chewy, and they last for days. You can use any flavor of jam.

Makes one 9" x 13" dish; cut to preferred size

1 ½ cups (342g) unsalted butter, melted and kept warm
3 cups (600g) granulated sugar
4 large eggs
1 tablespoon vanilla extract
1 tablespoon almond extract
3 ⅓ cups (395g) all-purpose flour, sifted
1 ½ teaspoons sea salt
½ cup (150g) seedless raspberry jam
¾ cup (65g) sliced almonds

Preheat oven to 350°. Lightly coat a 9" x 13" baking dish with nonstick spray and set aside.

In the bowl of a stand mixer fitted with the paddle attachment, combine melted butter and sugar on low speed until well blended. Add eggs one at a time, scraping the bowl after each addition. Add vanilla and almond extracts and mix until batter is smooth. Scrape bowl well.

Add flour and salt on the lowest speed until just combined. Remove bowl from stand mixer and finish folding in dry ingredients with a rubber spatula.

Pour half of the batter into prepared dish. Spread a layer of raspberry jam evenly onto the batter and cover with remaining batter. Top with sliced almonds.

Bake until almonds are golden, about 30 minutes, and then rotate dish and continue baking until a toothpick comes out clean, about 30 more minutes. Cool completely before cutting.

Photo at left: Fennel Blondies, top; Raspberry Foley Bars, middle; Brownies, bottom

BERRY CRUMBLE BAR

Teff is an ancient grain used in a lot of Ethiopian cooking. Cecilia uses it in this crumble because it's gluten-free, so it makes our gluten-sensitive customers very happy.
Gluten-free

Makes one 4″ x 12″ tart

1 recipe Teff Pâté à Sucre (*see page 25*)
Seeded Streusel (*see recipe below*)
2 tablespoons seedless raspberry jam
2 cups (240g) frozen blueberries
2 cups (195g) frozen blackberries
2 tablespoons granulated sugar
1 tablespoon cornstarch

Preheat oven to 375°. Make the Teff Pâté à Sucre recipe, but instead of fitting it into a round tart pan, press it into a 4″ x 12″ tea loaf pan. Cover it with parchment paper and pie weights. Blind bake until dough is firm, 15 to 20 minutes. Let cool 10 minutes. Remove parchment paper and pie weights and continue to bake 10 more minutes.

While shell is blind baking, make seeded streusel.

Use small offset spatula to spread jam into bottom of tart pan. In a medium mixing bowl, toss berries with sugar and cornstarch until well coated. Fill tart with berries, spreading them evenly over jam. Top with seeded streusel.

Bake for 30 minutes, rotate, and continue to bake until berry mixture is bubbling and jammy, about 20 more minutes. Cool 15 minutes before serving.

Seeded Streusel

1 tablespoon golden brown sugar
1½ tablespoons granulated sugar
¼ cup (40g) brown rice flour
2 tablespoons sunflower seeds
2 tablespoons sliced almonds
2 tablespoons old-fashioned rolled oats
2 tablespoons flaxseeds
2 tablespoons (28g) unsalted butter, cold, cut into ½-inch pieces
⅛ teaspoon sea salt

In the bowl of a stand mixer fitted with the paddle attachment, combine sugars, rice flour, sunflower seeds, almonds, oats, and flaxseeds on low speed. Add butter and salt. Continue to mix on low speed until mixture resembles wet sand, about 5 minutes. Check consistency by grabbing a handful of streusel: it should hold its shape for a few seconds and then crumble. Transfer to lidded container and refrigerate until tart is ready to assemble.

BROWN BUTTER APPLE NEWTONS

Fig Newtons were named for the city of Newton, Massachusetts. This is our spin on the cakey, textured cookie, made with brown butter apples instead of figs. Our version is also crunchy, similar to *cuccidati*, the Sicilian fig-filled cookie traditionally served at Christmastime.

Makes 24

Apple Filling

½ cup (100g) granulated sugar

1 vanilla bean, split lengthwise and scraped

4 large Granny Smith apples, peeled, cored, and sliced ¼ inch thick

¼ cup (57g) unsalted butter

Newton Dough

1 cup (228g) unsalted butter, softened

1 cup (200g) granulated sugar

3 egg whites, plus 1 more egg white, lightly beaten, for seal and wash

3 cups (360g) all-purpose flour, sifted, plus more for dusting

½ cup (110g) sanding or decorative sugar

Place sugar and vanilla bean pod and seeds in a large bowl. Rub vanilla pod with sugar to get all the seeds out. Add apples and toss to coat with vanilla sugar. Set aside and let macerate for 15 minutes.

Melt butter in a large saucepan over medium heat. Cook until butter foams and browns; a nutty aroma will develop. Add the apple-vanilla-sugar mixture. Stir with a heat-resistant rubber spatula and cook until apples are soft but still hold their shape and liquid thickens into a caramel, about 30 minutes. Remove from heat and let cool.

In the bowl of a stand mixer fitted with the paddle attachment, cream butter and sugar on low speed, about 30 seconds. Scrape bowl well with rubber spatula. Stream in 3 egg whites and mix on low speed for 30 seconds. Continue to mix on medium speed until well combined, about 15 seconds. Scrape bowl well. Add flour and mix on low speed until just incorporated, about 30 seconds. Finish incorporating flour into dough using a rubber spatula.

Transfer dough onto lightly floured parchment paper. Place another sheet of parchment paper on top and use a rolling pin to flatten dough into a ½-inch-thick rectangle. Chill in refrigerator until firm, at least 1 hour.

Pour cooled apple filling into food processor and purée. Pour purée into a disposable pastry bag. Set aside.

Remove Newton dough from refrigerator. Peel back parchment paper, lightly dust dough with flour to prevent sticking, and replace the paper. Flip dough rectangle over and do the same for the other side. Roll out the paper-covered dough into a 12″ x 14″ rectangle. Remove parchment paper on top. Use a chef's knife to cut the dough in half, yielding two 7″ x 12″ rectangles. Leave one on the parchment paper and transfer the other to fresh parchment paper. Arrange so the longer 12″ side is facing you, landscape style.

Use scissors to snip a ¼-inch opening on pastry bag of apple filling. Pipe the filling down the center of dough rectangle, moving across the 12-inch length. Divide filling evenly between two rectangles. The filling should measure 3″ x 12″. Fold bottom third of dough over the filling, like folding a letter. Because the dough will be a little sticky, lift the side of the parchment paper to help fold the bottom third over the filling.

Apply egg-white wash with pastry brush along the edge of the top third of dough. This will help seal the dough. Roll the center third of dough over the top third. Gently press along edges to seal. The assembled cookie log will resemble a chubby 3″ x 12″ rectangle. Wrap with parchment so the log sits on its seam. Repeat with remaining dough rectangle. Freeze cookie logs overnight or until firm, at least 1 hour. Frozen cookie dough will keep in an airtight container for up to 2 weeks.

Preheat oven to 375°. Use a chef's knife to slice cookies 1 inch wide on a bias. Each log will yield 12 cookies. Apply egg wash to tops of cookies and dip into sanding sugar. Place cookies, evenly spaced at least 1 inch apart, on parchment-lined sheet pans. Bake, rotating halfway through, until edges are golden brown, about 16 minutes.

WALNUT RUGELACH

I love how flaky and nutty these are. Bake them well so they crisp up nicely.

Makes 12

1 recipe Cream Cheese Dough (*see page 22*), thawed if frozen
All-purpose flour, for dusting
½ cup (106g) golden brown sugar, packed
½ cup (114g) unsalted butter, softened
2 teaspoons honey
1 teaspoon bourbon
1 teaspoon vanilla extract
½ teaspoon ground cinnamon
1 teaspoon sea salt
1 cup (140g) walnuts, coarsely ground
1 egg, for wash
¼ cup (55g) sanding or turbinado sugar, for sprinkling

Place parchment paper lightly dusted with flour on work surface. Unwrap dough and place it onto paper. Lightly dust dough with flour and place another sheet of parchment paper on top. Use rolling pin to roll dough between the sheets of parchment paper until it measures 12″ x 20″ and is ⅛ inch thick. Cut rectangle in half to make two 10″ x 12″ rectangles. If dough is too soft to handle well, transfer onto parchment-lined sheet pans and chill in refrigerator until firm, 10 to 15 minutes.

In the bowl of a stand mixer fitted with the paddle attachment, combine brown sugar, butter, honey, bourbon, vanilla extract, cinnamon, and salt. Add ground walnuts and mix until combined.

Transfer dough to work surface, positioning it so the 12-inch side is facing you. Use a small offset spatula to spread filling evenly over rectangles. Roll dough into a log and use a chef's knife to cut into 2-inch wide rugelach. Place 1 inch apart onto parchment-lined sheet pan and freeze until firm, about 1 hour.

Preheat oven to 375°. In a small bowl, beat egg. Apply egg wash with pastry brush, and then sprinkle with sanding sugar. Bake, rotating halfway through, until golden brown, about 30 minutes.

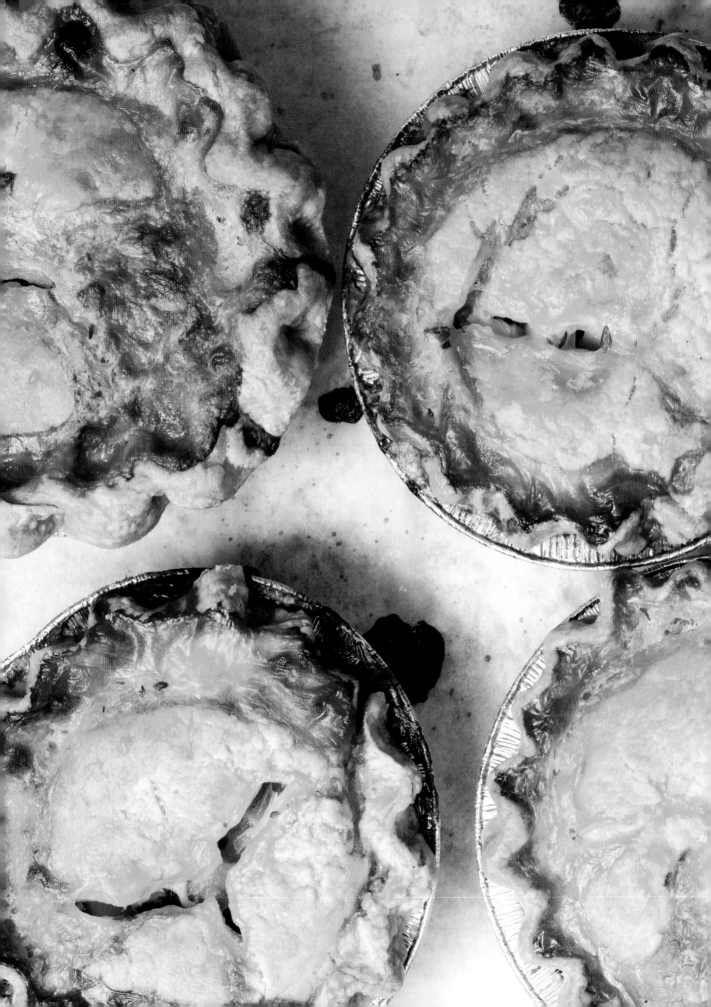

SAVORIES

Going into New York City on Sundays as a kid always meant stopping for a soft pretzel from a street vendor. The aromas of brown mustard and dough fill my thoughts as I write this. The pretzels were warm, salty, and probably the best thing I had ever had at the age of five. I've been a lifelong pretzel fan ever since; any shape, size, or texture will do.

   Our pretzel roll is a huge craving for many of our fantastic customers, thank goodness! So are many of the savory recipes in this chapter.

BIALYS

Growing up in New Jersey made me crazy for bagels at a young age. We would ride bikes to Sonny's Bagels on South Orange Avenue and spend fifteen cents for the most wonderful warm, fresh, chewy bagels. Sonny's is still there, and I take my kids there when we visit Grammy. Nowadays I order a bialy, which is basically a Polish bagel that's baked, not boiled. Sonny's makes the best onion bialy.

Note: Poolish is not a typo for polish or Polish—it's the precise word for the fairly wet sponge that makes yeast activation happen. Start the day before, because the dough needs to proof overnight in the refrigerator.

Makes 12

Poolish
¼ cup (50g) grapeseed oil
1¼ teaspoons active dry yeast
4¾ cups (570g) bread flour
2½ cups (555g) lukewarm water

Bialys
¾ teaspoon active dry yeast
7 tablespoons (97g) water
4½ (540g) cups bread flour
1 tablespoon malt syrup
¼ cup + 1½ teaspoons (56g) grapeseed oil
2 tablespoons sea salt
1 egg, beaten
Toppings of your choice

In a large bowl, mix yeast, bread flour, and water together to make the poolish. Cover with plastic wrap and let sit at room temperature 2 hours. It will double in volume and be bubbly.

Lightly brush oil onto parchment-lined half-sheet pans. Set aside.

When poolish is ready, place yeast and water in the bowl of a stand mixer and whisk by hand to dissolve yeast. Add risen poolish, bread flour, malt syrup, oil, and salt. Fit the dough hook on the mixer and mix on the lowest speed until dough is smooth, about 6 minutes.

Divide dough into 12 4-ounce balls, forming with clawed hands so a seam forms on the underside of each ball. Transfer onto oiled parchment-lined pans. Cover with plastic wrap and proof overnight in refrigerator.

Preheat oven to 425°. Remove bialys from refrigerator and make a 3-inch indentation in the center of each. Using a pastry brush, coat each bialy with beaten egg. Add toppings of your choice—perhaps bacon and cheddar, or tomato with parmesan and basil, or caramelized onion and shredded Swiss. (The photo at left shows bialys topped with onion, Swiss, and crispy quinoa.) Treat it like a little pizza. Make sure the edges get love, too!

Bake, rotating halfway through, until golden brown, about 15 minutes.

To add steam, you can spray water into the oven, but that's optional.

BACON CHEDDAR SCONES

This is a classic combination. They're even yummier when dipped in sour cream while they're still warm!

Makes 16

4 1/4 cups (510g) all-purpose flour, plus more for dusting

1 tablespoon + 1 1/2 teaspoons baking powder

2 teaspoons sea salt

2 tablespoons chives, chopped

1 teaspoon onion powder

1 1/2 cups (342g) unsalted butter, cut into 1/4-inch cubes and chilled

3/4 cup + 2 tablespoons (210g) heavy whipping cream

4 large eggs

5 slices cooked bacon, chopped

1 cup (115g) shredded cheddar

Preheat oven to 375°. Line a sheet pan with parchment paper. In the bowl of a stand mixer fitted with the paddle attachment, combine flour, baking powder, salt, chives, and onion powder on low speed. Gradually add butter and continue to mix until pea-size lumps form.

Add cream and eggs all at once. Mix on low speed for 30 seconds until just combined. Add bacon and cheddar and continue mixing for 30 seconds until just combined. Do not overmix; dough should be shaggy, with some dry bits.

Transfer dough onto a lightly floured surface and pat into a 12-inch square that is 1 inch thick. Use a chef's knife to cut into 16 3-inch squares. Transfer scones to parchment-lined sheet pan, spaced 1 inch apart. Freeze until firm, at least 1 hour, or overnight.

Bake, rotating halfway through, until golden brown, about 30 minutes.

ONION SWISS SCONES

Swiss cheese and onions make for a timeless combination that's one of my favorites. These scones are delicious with a poached egg or two.

Makes 16

4 1/4 cups (510g) all-purpose flour, plus more for dusting

1 tablespoon + 1 1/2 teaspoons baking powder

2 teaspoons sea salt

1 teaspoon onion powder

1/2 teaspoon granulated garlic

1/4 teaspoon ground cumin

1 1/2 cups (342g) unsalted butter, cut into 1/4-inch cubes and chilled

1 cup (240g) heavy whipping cream

4 large eggs

1 cup (200g) caramelized onions

1 1/2 cups (175g) shredded Swiss cheese

Preheat oven to 375°. Line a sheet pan with parchment paper. In the bowl of a stand mixer fitted with the paddle attachment, combine flour, baking powder, salt, onion powder, granulated garlic, and cumin and mix on low speed. Gradually add butter and mix until pea-size lumps form.

Add cream and eggs all at once. Mix on low speed for 30 seconds until just combined. Add onions and cheese and mix on low speed for 30 seconds until just combined. Do not overmix; dough should be shaggy, with some dry bits.

Transfer dough onto a lightly floured surface and pat into a 12-inch square that is 1 inch thick. Use a chef's knife to cut into 16 3-inch squares. Transfer scones onto parchment-lined sheet pan, leaving 1 inch between each. Freeze until firm, at least 1 hour, or overnight.

Bake, rotating halfway through, until golden brown, about 30 minutes.

BAKING POWDER BISCUITS

A traditional biscuit that's delicious with jam or gravy. Quinoa adds a snappy texture.

Makes 12

3 1/2 cups (420g) all-purpose flour, plus more for dusting
1 1/2 tablespoons baking powder
3/4 teaspoon sea salt
1/4 cup + 2 tablespoons (75g) granulated sugar
3/4 cup (171g) unsalted butter, cut into 1/4-inch cubes and chilled
1 cup (240g) heavy whipping cream, divided
3/4 cup (168g) buttermilk
1 egg

In the bowl of a stand mixer fitted with the paddle attachment, combine flour, baking powder, salt, and sugar on low speed. Gradually add butter, mixing on low speed until pea-size lumps form, about 2 minutes. Add 3/4 cup (180g) cream, buttermilk, and egg and mix until dough just comes together. Dough will feel tacky and supple but not sticky.

Transfer dough to a lightly floured surface. Gently pat into a 1-inch-thick rectangle. Do not overwork. Use a chef's knife to cut dough into 12 2-inch squares. Place biscuits onto parchment-lined sheet pan. Use a pastry brush to apply remaining 1/4 cup (60g) cream (as a wash) on top of each biscuit. Freeze until firm, at least 1 hour, or overnight. They will keep in an airtight container in the freezer for up to 2 weeks.

Preheat oven to 375°. Bake, rotating halfway through, until golden brown, about 25 minutes.

Variations

Savory: Omit the sugar.

Quinoa (*photographed at left*): Reduce all-purpose flour to 3 cups plus 3 tablespoons (380g), add 3 tablespoons (20g) whole-wheat flour and 3/4 cup (120g) cooked quinoa, and omit the sugar. Sprinkle with salt after the cream wash and bake as directed.

POTATO BACON HERB BISCUITS

Potato, bacon, and biscuits...all together! This is a great way to used leftover bacon and potatoes—just add a scrambled egg and you've got breakfast. These keep well in the freezer, too.

Makes 15

3 medium or 2 large (400g) Yukon gold potatoes
Olive or grapeseed oil for roasting potatoes
4 1/2 cups (540g) all-purpose flour, plus more for dusting
1 tablespoon + 2 teaspoons baking powder
2 teaspoons sea salt
1/2 cup (30g) chopped dill, packed
1/4 cup (12g) chopped chives, packed
1/4 cup (24g) chopped parsley, packed
1 1/2 cups (342g) butter, cut into 1/2-inch pieces and chilled
4 large eggs
3/4 cup + 1 tablespoon (195g) heavy whipping cream
5 slices bacon, cooked and chopped
1 egg, whisked, for wash
1 tablespoon Maldon sea salt

Preheat oven to 375°. Rub potatoes with oil and roast until fork-tender, about 25 minutes. Smash with a large spoon or fork and set aside.

In the bowl of a stand mixer fitted with the paddle attachment, combine flour, baking powder, salt, dill, chives, and parsley on lowest speed. Gradually add butter and mix at the lowest speed until butter is well coated with flour and pea-size lumps form, about 2 minutes.

Add eggs and cream. Mix until just incorporated, but no longer. Add potatoes and bacon and mix on low speed until just incorporated. Dough should be shaggy with some dry bits.

Transfer dough onto a lightly floured surface and pat into a 1-inch-thick rectangle. Use a chef's knife to cut dough into 15 2 1/2-inch squares. Transfer to a parchment-lined sheet pan, spacing biscuits 1/2 inch apart. Use a pastry brush to apply egg wash. Sprinkle biscuits with Maldon salt and freeze until firm, at least 1 hour, or overnight. They will keep in an airtight container in the freezer for up to 2 weeks.

Bake, rotating halfway through, until golden, about 30 minutes.

CORN SCALLION SRIRACHA BISCUITS

Savory with a little heat—we love Sriracha! These were inspired by Diep Tran's blistered corn, which she serves at Good Girl Dinette in L.A.'s Highland Park neighborhood. Note that fish sauce can be found in many markets, but our favorite, Red Boat, is less commonly seen; you can get it at Sur la Table or on Amazon.

Makes 16

4 1/4 cups (510g) all-purpose flour, plus more for dusting
1 tablespoon + 1 teaspoon baking powder
2 teaspoons sea salt
1 1/2 cups (342g) unsalted butter, cut into 1/4-inch cubes and chilled
4 large eggs
3/4 cup + 2 tablespoons (210g) heavy whipping cream
1 tablespoon fish sauce
2 cups (225g) frozen corn kernels
1/2 cup (48g) green onions, chopped

Sriracha Glaze
1/4 cup (57g) unsalted butter, softened
2 tablespoons Sriracha
1 tablespoon + 1 teaspoon fish sauce
1 1/2 teaspoons granulated sugar

In the bowl of a stand mixer fitted with the paddle attachment, combine flour, baking powder, and salt on low speed. Gradually add butter and mix at low speed until pea-size lumps form.

Add eggs, cream, and fish sauce, mixing on low speed until just combined, about 30 seconds. Add corn and green onions, mixing on lowest speed for 30 seconds, until just combined but no longer. Dough should be shaggy with some dry bits.

Transfer dough onto lightly floured surface and pat into a 12-inch square that is 1 inch thick. Use a chef's knife or metal bench scraper to cut into 3-inch squares. Transfer biscuits onto a parchment-lined sheet pan, leaving 1 inch between each. Freeze until firm, at least 1 hour, or overnight. They will keep in an airtight container in the freezer for up to 2 weeks.

Preheat oven to 375°. Bake, rotating halfway through, until golden brown, about 30 minutes.

While biscuits are baking, make the Sriracha glaze. Whisk together butter, Sriracha, fish sauce, and sugar in a small saucepan over medium heat. When biscuits come out of the oven, apply glaze with a pastry brush.

SAVORY MUFFINS

Inspired by William Werner of Craftsman and Wolves, this savory muffin has it all, including an egg!

Makes 6

2 eggs, room temperature
1/4 cup + 1 1/2 tablespoons (69g) grapeseed oil
1/2 cup (112g) buttermilk
2 2/3 cups (314g) all-purpose flour, sifted
2 teaspoons baking powder
1 teaspoon baking soda
1 teaspoon sea salt
1/2 teaspoon freshly ground pepper
1/8 teaspoon ground cumin
2/3 cup (100g) shredded zucchini
2 medium shallots, roasted and smashed (*see instructions below*)
3 cloves garlic, roasted and smashed (*see instructions below*)
2 cups (230g) shredded cheddar, divided
6 large eggs, cold

Preheat oven to 375° and line a 6-cup muffin tin with muffin liners.

In the bowl of a stand mixer fitted with the whisk attachment, beat eggs on medium speed for 10 seconds. Reduce speed to low and stream in oil. Add buttermilk and mix on low speed until just combined. Add flour, baking powder, baking soda, salt, pepper, and cumin all at once. Mix on low speed until just combined, about 15 seconds. Batter will be shaggy.

Remove bowl from mixer. Fold in zucchini, shallots, garlic, and 1 cup (115g) cheddar with rubber spatula.

Spoon 1/2 cup batter into each muffin mold. Use a spoon to press batter along sides of muffin liners to create a large crater for egg. Use cold eggs only! Crack an egg into each crater. Sprinkle liberally with remaining 1 cup (115g) cheddar.

Bake, rotating halfway through, until toothpick in the muffin part comes out clean, about 30 minutes. Serve warm.

To Roast Shallots and Garlic

Preheat oven to 375°. Peel shallots and garlic, place in a small baking dish, and cover with extra-virgin olive oil. Cover with foil and bake until both are fork-tender, about 20 minutes. Let cool and strain. Discard oil or save and use flavored oil to season vegetables, as a shallot-garlic-based salad dressing, or as part of a marinade for meats.

BUTTERMILK PRETZEL ROLLS

The aroma of soft pretzels and roasting chestnuts from a street cart in New York City meant a great day at Central Park or a museum visit. Memories from childhood are so powerful and comforting. Making these pretzel rolls every day in the café keeps those memories alive.

Makes 16

Dough

2 tablespoons (18g) active dry yeast

1 1/2 cups (333g) warm water, 95° to 110°

1/2 cup + 2 tablespoons (140g) buttermilk

2 tablespoons + 1 teaspoon grapeseed oil

5 cups (600g) bread flour, plus more for dusting

1/3 cup (71g) golden brown sugar, packed

2 teaspoons granulated sugar

1 tablespoon sea salt

1/2 cup (100g) grapeseed oil, plus more to coat bowl

3 tablespoons pretzel salt or coarse sea salt

Poaching Liquid

6 tablespoons (108g) baking soda

1 cup (213g) golden brown sugar, packed

3 cups (666g) water

Place yeast and warm water in a small bowl and whisk until yeast dissolves. Set aside until foamy, about 5 minutes. Add buttermilk and oil. Set wet mixture aside.

In the bowl of a stand mixer fitted with the dough hook, combine flour, sugars, and salt on lowest speed for 15 seconds. Add wet mixture all at once and mix on lowest speed until dough is smooth and tacky, 15 to 20 minutes.

Lightly coat a medium bowl with grapeseed oil. Transfer dough to the oiled bowl. Flip the dough so it is coated with oil. Cover with plastic wrap and let sit at room temperature until doubled in volume, about 1 hour.

Line 2 sheet pans with parchment paper and brush paper with oil. Turn dough onto lightly floured surface. Divide dough into 16 even portions, each about the size of a tennis ball. Roll each portion into a 6- to 7-inch rope. Tie each rope into a simple knot. Set pretzel rolls onto the sheet pans.

Preheat oven to 375°. To make poaching liquid, combine baking soda, brown sugar, and water in a large saucepan over medium heat. Bring the mixture to a gentle boil.

Set up a small bowl with 1/2 cup grapeseed oil, a pastry brush, and a small bowl of pretzel salt.

Once poaching liquid foams, begin poaching. Use a slotted or perforated spoon to submerge 3 pretzel rolls for 8 seconds. Remove from saucepan and place onto sheet pan, leaving at least 1 1/2 inches of space between each roll. Brush each roll with oil and sprinkle with a pinch of pretzel salt. Continue to poach the remaining pretzel rolls in same manner.

Bake poached pretzel rolls until golden, about 12 minutes. Rotate pan and continue baking until darker golden brown, about 12 more minutes.

Tip: Specialty ingredients, such as the pretzel salt above, can be found at Whole Foods, Sprouts, and other quality markets, or order online from Bob's Red Mill.

BUTTERMILK PRETZEL DOGS

Chewy pretzel and salty dog! I always need more brown mustard.

Makes 16

1 recipe Buttermilk Pretzel Dough (*see page 209*)
1 cup (280g) whole-grain mustard
16 hot dogs

Make pretzel dough using method described on page 209. Portion dough into 16 3″ x 5″ rectangles. Use a metal bench scraper or knife to cut 5 1-inch slits on each of the long sides of each dough rectangle, leaving the central 2 inches uncut for the hot dog to rest on. Spread 1 tablespoon mustard down that 2-inch middle length. Place hot dog atop the mustard. Starting with the right side, pick up the first slit at the top and cross it over the hot dog and press on the left. Pick up the first slit at the top on the left side and cross it over the hot dog and press on the right. You're creating a faux braid by crisscrossing the dough, much like lacing up sneakers.

Poach and bake pretzel dogs using the method described on page 209.

ZUCCHINI GOAT CHEESE QUICHE

Our best-selling quiche.

Makes one 10-inch quiche

1/2 recipe (about 500g) Brisée Dough (*see page 22*)
9 large eggs
1 1/2 cups (353g) whole milk
1 cup (240g) heavy whipping cream
1 teaspoon sea salt
1/4 teaspoon freshly ground pepper
1 cup (150g) shredded zucchini
1 tablespoon chopped parsley
1/4 cup (50g) goat cheese

Lightly coat a 10-inch pie pan with nonstick spray and set aside. Take out chilled brisée dough. Lightly flour work surface and roll dough out into a 15-inch circle that is 1/8 inch thick. Gently fold in half and then fold in half again, so dough is quartered. Transfer dough to pie pan with the folded corner in the center. Unfold dough, gently laying it into pan. Press dough into bottom of pie pan and tuck into edges and sides of the pan to prevent air gaps. Roll dough overhang under itself to create a crust, and flute the edge. Freeze formed pie shell for at least 1 hour.

In the bowl of a stand mixer fitted with the whisk attachment, mix eggs on medium speed for 1 minute. Stream in milk and cream and whisk on low speed for 1 minute. Add salt and pepper and mix for 1 more minute. This is the quiche custard. Use immediately or store in an airtight container in the refrigerator for up to 3 days.

Preheat oven to 375°. To blind bake the shell, remove chilled brisée shell from freezer, line with parchment, and top with pie weights or dried beans. Place on a sheet pan. Bake until crust is golden and opaque, 25 to 30 minutes. Remove parchment paper and pie weights and continue to bake, uncovered, until bottom of shell is opaque and light golden brown, another 10 to 15 minutes.

Decrease oven temperature to 350°.

Fill blind-baked shell with an even layer of shredded zucchini. Add parsley and dollop with tablespoons of goat cheese. Fill with quiche custard, leaving 1/4 inch space below fluted edge. Bake until custard forms a skin, about 30 minutes. Rotate pan and continue baking until custard is set, about 30 more minutes. To test doneness, insert a paring knife into the center. Custard should be soft and creamy but not liquid. Let cool for at least 1 hour before serving.

CHICKEN POT PIES

Flaky brisée dough makes these individual pies irresistible. Make them by the dozen and store them in the freezer for an easy dinner.

Makes 4

¼ cup (57g) unsalted butter
½ cup (60g) all-purpose flour
1½ cups (345g) vegetable broth, room temperature
1½ cups (353g) whole milk, room temperature
1½ teaspoons sea salt, divided, plus more to taste
6 sprigs thyme
2 tablespoons grapeseed oil
½ cup (95g) carrots, peeled and chopped
½ cup (75g) russet potato, peeled and chopped
⅓ cup (70g) chopped onion
1 cup (45g) chopped kale
¼ teaspoon freshly ground black pepper
½ cup (70g) frozen peas
1 cup (135g) shredded cooked chicken
1 teaspoon chopped fresh thyme
1 tablespoon chopped fresh parsley
1 recipe Brisée Dough (*see page 22*)
1 egg, whisked, for wash
Maldon sea salt, for sprinkling

Place butter in a medium saucepan over medium-low heat. Once butter is melted, whisk in flour to make a blond roux, or paste. Gradually stream and whisk in vegetable broth until well incorporated. Whisk in milk. Add ½ teaspoon salt and thyme sprigs. Bring sauce to a simmer, whisking constantly, until mixture thickens to nappé, or coats the back of the spoon. Remove from heat and strain into a large bowl. Discard thyme. Set aside.

Place a large sauté pan over medium heat. Once pan is hot, add oil. Add carrots and potatoes and sweat or cook the vegetables until fork-tender. Add onion and continue to cook until onion is translucent. Add kale and cook until it wilts. Season with 1 teaspoon salt and ¼ teaspoon pepper. Remove from heat and fold cooked vegetables into sauce that you've set aside in the bowl. Fold in peas, chicken, thyme, and parsley. Taste and add salt and/or pepper if needed. Set aside.

Remove 2 disks chilled brisée dough from refrigerator and roll each out to a ³⁄₈-inch thickness. Lightly coat 4 small, deep pie pans or other dishes with nonstick spray. Cut each rolled-out piece of dough into quarters; you will have 8 pieces. Press one into the bottom of each of the 4 tins. Scoop 1½ cups filling into each brisée shell. Cover with another layer of dough and press to seal edges. Use scissors to trim excess dough, leaving a ½-inch overhang. Crimp or form edge as you like. Freeze 30 minutes.

Preheat oven to 375°. Use pastry brush to apply egg wash to the top of each pie. Sprinkle with Maldon salt. Use a paring knife to cut a ½-inch slit in the center of each top. Place pies onto sheet pan and bake, rotating halfway through, until crust is golden brown and sauce bubbles, about 1 hour.

ALSATIAN ONION TART

Caramelized onion and parmesan make a flavorful, savory tart that's good for breakfast, lunch, and dinner.

Makes one 8 1/2-inch tart

1/2 recipe (about 500g) Brisée Dough (*see page 22*)
1 tablespoon grapeseed oil
1 medium yellow onion, julienned
1 teaspoon sea salt, divided
1/4 teaspoon chopped fresh thyme
1/8 teaspoon ground cumin
2 large eggs
1/2 cup (120g) heavy whipping cream
1/4 teaspoon freshly ground pepper
1/2 cup (55g) shredded parmesan

Lightly coat an 8 1/2-inch tart pan with nonstick spray. Take out chilled brisée and roll out until dough is 3/8 inch thick. Press dough into tin, making sure to press into edges to remove any air bubbles. Freeze 30 minutes. Preheat oven to 375°.

Place a large sauté pan over medium heat. Once pan is hot, add oil. Add onion and cook until translucent. Season with 1/2 teaspoon salt. Stir and continue to cook until onions are golden brown and taste sweet. Add thyme and cumin. Remove from heat and set aside.

Lightly coat formed tart shell with nonstick spray and top with parchment paper and pie weights or dried beans. Place on sheet pan and blind bake 20 minutes. Remove parchment paper and pie weights. Continue to bake until shell is light golden brown and opaque, about 15 more minutes. Let cool 10 minutes.

In a large bowl, whisk eggs until broken but no longer. Do not incorporate too much air. Whisk in cream until combined. Season with remaining 1/2 teaspoon salt and 1/4 teaspoon pepper. This is your custard.

Spread an even layer of caramelized onions on tart shell. Sprinkle with parmesan. Pour custard over onions and parmesan. Bake, rotating halfway through, until tart is golden and custard is set, 15 to 20 minutes.

POTATO TART

Potatoes baked in cream! Also delicious if you add bacon.

Makes one 9-inch tart

1/2 recipe (about 500g) Brisée Dough (*see page 22*)
5 cloves garlic, peeled
1 cup (240g) heavy whipping cream, divided
2 russet potatoes, peeled and sliced 1/8 inch thick
1 1/2 teaspoons sea salt
1/4 teaspoon freshly ground pepper

Remove chilled brisée from refrigerator and roll out to a 3/8-inch thickness. Lightly coat a 9-inch tart pan with nonstick spray. Press dough into tart pan, being sure to press into corners and edges to remove air gaps. Freeze 30 minutes. Preheat oven to 375°.

To make garlic cream, place garlic and 1/2 cup (120g) cream in small saucepan over high heat and scald the cream. Let cool. Pour into blender and blend until puréed. Set aside.

Lightly spray formed brisée shell with nonstick spray, line with parchment paper, and top with pie weights or dried beans. Place on sheet pan and blind bake 20 minutes. Remove parchment paper and pie weights and continue baking until shell is golden and opaque, about 10 more minutes. Let cool 10 minutes.

Use a small offset spatula to spread 3 tablespoons garlic cream onto tart shell. Arrange potatoes on tart in a rosette. Season with 1/2 teaspoon salt and sprinkle of black pepper. Spread another 3 tablespoons garlic cream on top. Arrange a second layer of potatoes. Season with salt and pepper. Spread remaining garlic cream on top. Season with salt and pepper. Pour remaining 1/2 cup (120g) cream over the top.

Bake, rotating halfway through, until the top is golden brown and bubbly and potatoes are fork-tender, about 1 hour.

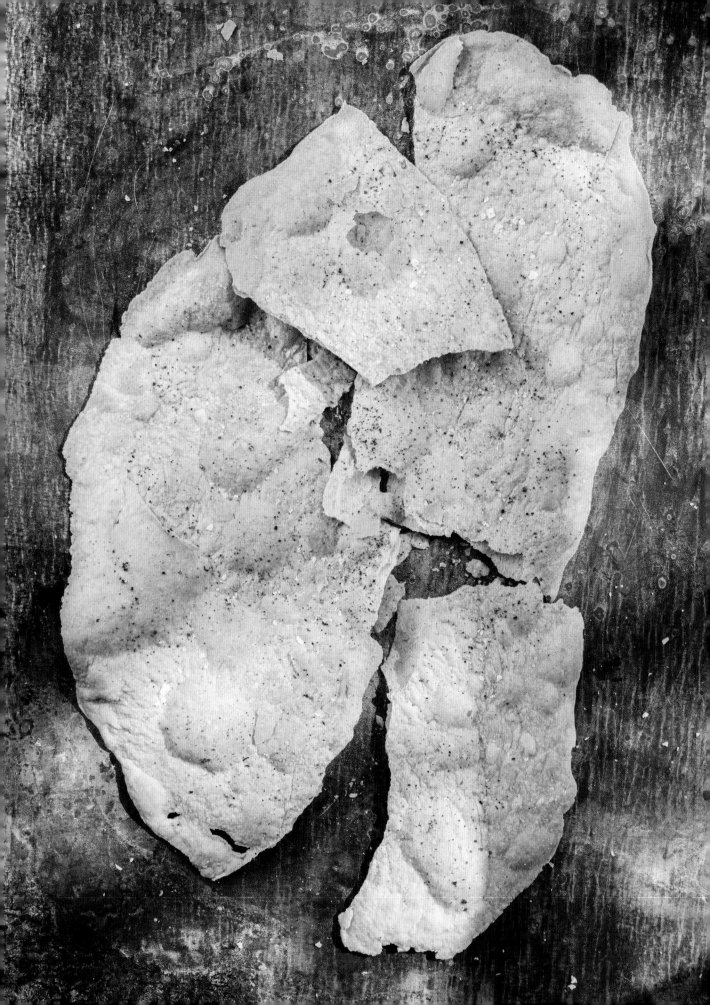

BUTTERMILK FIVE-SPICE CRACKERS

I could eat these crackers for days! Crunchy and salty, with a little five-spice flavor, too. Roll them nice and thin!

Makes 4 large crackers

1 3/4 cups (210g) all-purpose flour
1 tablespoon granulated sugar
1/2 teaspoon baking powder
1/2 teaspoon sea salt, plus more to taste
2 teaspoons Chinese Five-Spice Powder (*see recipe below*)
5 tablespoons (71g) unsalted butter, cut into 1/4-inch pieces and chilled
3/4 cup (168g) buttermilk
1/4 cup (50g) grapeseed oil
Freshly ground pepper to taste

Place flour, sugar, baking powder, 1/2 teaspoon salt, and five-spice powder in a food processor and blend. Add cold butter and continue to blend until mixture resembles coarse meal. Add buttermilk and continue to blend until dough pulls away from the side and forms a ball.

Wrap dough with plastic wrap and chill in the refrigerator at least 30 minutes.

Preheat oven to 375°. Divide chilled dough into 4 even pieces. Place each ball of chilled dough between two sheets of parchment paper and roll out to a 1/8-inch thickness. Transfer to a sheet pan. Use pastry brush to apply a thin coat of grapeseed oil atop the dough. Season to taste with salt and pepper.

Bake, rotating halfway through, until golden brown, about 18 minutes.

Chinese Five-Spice Powder

1 teaspoon star anise, toasted
1 teaspoon fennel seeds, toasted
1 teaspoon Sichuan peppers, toasted
1 teaspoon ground cinnamon
1/8 teaspoon ground cloves

Place toasted star anise, fennel seeds, and Sichuan peppers in a spice grinder and grind into a fine powder. Combine with cinnamon and cloves. Store in an airtight container.

CHEDDAR CRACKERS

Crisp and flaky, these crackers make a good gift during the holidays.

Makes 24

1 cup (228g) unsalted butter, cut into 1/4-inch cubes and chilled

1 3/4 teaspoons sea salt

1/4 teaspoon ground cayenne pepper

1 teaspoon freshly ground black pepper

1 teaspoon chopped chives

1 cup (170g) shredded cheddar

3 cups (360g) all-purpose flour

In the bowl of a stand mixer fitted with the paddle attachment, cream together butter, salt, cayenne, black pepper, and chives on low speed for 1 minute. Scrape bowl well with rubber spatula. Add cheddar and flour and mix on low speed until combined.

Form dough into a rectangle. Wrap in plastic wrap and chill in the refrigerator at least 30 minutes.

Place chilled dough between two sheets of parchment paper and roll out to a 1/8-inch thickness. Transfer the dough and the bottom layer of parchment paper to a sheet pan. Chill in the refrigerator until firm, about 15 minutes.

Preheat oven to 375°. Use a 2-inch-round cutter to cut crackers. Arrange them on a parchment-lined sheet pan spaced 1/2 inch apart. Chill in the freezer 10 minutes before baking.

Bake, rotating halfway through, until crackers are golden brown, about 22 minutes.

Variation: **Oat**

Substitute 1/2 cup (50g) rolled oats for 1/2 cup (60g) all-purpose flour.

BUCKWHEAT CRACKERS

Miso adds an extra bit of savory flavor to these nutty crackers.

Makes 24

3/4 cup (85g) whole-wheat flour

1/2 cup (60g) all-purpose flour

1/2 teaspoon sea salt

1/4 cup (58g) buckwheat groats

1/2 cup (114g) unsalted butter, cut into 1/4-inch cubes and chilled

1 tablespoon yellow miso

1/4 cup + 1 tablespoon (63g) extra-virgin olive oil

1/4 cup (55g) cold water

1 egg, whisked, for wash

2 tablespoons flaxseeds

2 tablespoons sesame seeds

Place whole-wheat flour, all-purpose flour, salt, and buckwheat groats in a food processor and blend. Add cold butter, miso, and olive oil. Continue to blend until mixture resembles coarse meal. Add cold water and continue to mix until dough pulls away from the side to form a ball.

Form dough into a rectangle. Wrap with plastic wrap and let chill in the refrigerator at least 30 minutes.

Unwrap chilled dough and place between two sheets of parchment paper. Roll out to a 1/8-inch thickness. Transfer the dough and the bottom layer of parchment paper to a sheet pan and chill in the refrigerator until firm, about 15 minutes.

Preheat oven to 375°. Use a 2-inch-round cutter to cut crackers. Transfer to a parchment-lined sheet pan, leaving 1/2 inch between each cracker. Use a pastry brush to apply egg wash, then sprinkle flaxseeds and sesame seeds on top. Chill in freezer 10 minutes before baking.

Bake, rotating halfway through, until crackers are golden brown, about 20 minutes.

GLAZED NUTS

Perfect for a holiday gift.
Gluten-free

Makes 10 cups

1 egg white
2 teaspoons sea salt
3/4 cup (94g) powdered sugar
1/2 teaspoon ground cayenne pepper
1 teaspoon ground cinnamon
2 tablespoons coarsely chopped
   rosemary
2 cups (256g) raw pecans
2 cups (260g) raw cashews
2 cups (284g) raw almonds
2 cups (256g) raw walnuts

Preheat oven to 350°. Line 2 sheet pans
with parchment paper and lightly coat
with nonstick spray.

In a large bowl, whisk together egg
white, salt, powdered sugar, cayenne
pepper, cinnamon, and rosemary. Add
pecans, cashews, almonds, and walnuts
and mix until well coated.

Divide nuts evenly between 2 sheet
pans, and spread them into a single layer.
Bake until glaze is opaque white and
begins to dry, about 12 minutes, then stir
nuts and rotate pans. Continue baking
until nuts are golden brown, about 10
more minutes. Cool completely before
storing in airtight container. Nuts will
keep in an airtight container for up to
2 weeks.

SWEETS

I've always loved candy! Butterfinger, Baby Ruth, Reese's Peanut Butter Cups . . . when I was growing up in Maplewood, New Jersey, Halloween was my favorite holiday. There was always one amazing house that gave out full-size candy bars! A roll of pennies was super-great, too. It made our pillowcases feel heavy, like we were hauling a really big load of candy. I also loved salt water taffy from the Jersey Shore, licorice from Germany, and red fish from Sweden. I could go on and on. Instead, I'll share some favorite sweet treats.

CARAMEL CORN

Just try to stop yourself.
Gluten-free

Makes 12 cups

¼ cup (50g) grapeseed oil
½ cup (105g) popcorn kernels, unpopped
¾ cup (171g) unsalted butter
1½ cups (320g) golden brown sugar, packed
¼ cup + 2 tablespoons (90g) corn syrup
1 teaspoon Fleur de Sel de Guérande salt
1 teaspoon vanilla extract
½ teaspoon baking soda

Preheat oven to 250°. Line 2 sheet pans with parchment paper and lightly coat with nonstick spray.

Heat a large stockpot or saucepan over medium heat. Add oil to heat for 30 seconds. Add popcorn kernels and place lid on top. Shake pot occasionally to prevent the kernels from burning. Shake more vigorously as kernels begin to pop. Pour popped corn into large mixing bowl to cool.

Melt butter in a medium saucepan. Add brown sugar and corn syrup and continue to cook over medium heat until sugars dissolve. Stir with rubber spatula to make sure caramel is smooth. Increase heat to medium high to boil and bubble for 3 to 4 minutes.

Remove saucepan from heat, add salt, vanilla extract, and baking soda, and stir with rubber spatula. Caramel will bubble and lighten. Quickly pour over popped corn and stir to coat.

Divide caramel corn evenly between the 2 sheet pans and spread into a single layer. Bake for 15 minutes and rotate pans. Caramel will be bubbling and starting to dry out. Stir the popcorn and bake until caramel corn is golden brown and dry, about 15 more minutes. Cool completely before storing in airtight container. Popcorn will keep for up to 1 week.

Variation: **Curry**
Add 2 tablespoons Madras curry powder and 1 teaspoon orange zest to caramel.

MARSHMALLOWS

These are super fun to flavor and shape any way you want. They're a staple at the candy shop, and they make great gifts.

Gluten-free

Makes 48

1 1/2 cups (333g) water, divided
1/4 cup (40g) powdered gelatin
2 1/2 cups (500g) granulated sugar
1 cup (319g) corn syrup
1/2 vanilla bean, split lengthwise and scraped
2 teaspoons vanilla extract
1/4 cup (31g) powdered sugar
1/4 cup (28g) cornstarch

Pour 3/4 cup (167g) water in the bowl of a stand mixer fitted with the whisk attachment and sprinkle with gelatin to bloom (allow the gelatin to absorb liquid and expand), 5 to 8 minutes.

Place 3/4 cup (167g) water, sugar, and corn syrup in a large saucepan and bring to a boil. Clip a candy thermometer to saucepan. When temperature of syrup reaches 240°, remove from heat.

Mix water-gelatin mixture on low speed and slowly stream in hot syrup down the sides of the mixing bowl. Add vanilla bean seeds and vanilla extract. When syrup is fully incorporated, increase mixer speed to high. Whip mixture until thick and room temperature, 12 to 15 minutes.

While marshmallow mixture is whipping, prepare 9" x 13" pan by coating it with nonstick spray. Combine powdered sugar and cornstarch in a medium bowl. Generously dust coated pan with 1/2 of the powdered sugar-cornstarch mixture and set aside.

Coat a plastic bowl scraper and your hand with nonstick spray. Pour and scrape marshmallow mixture into prepared pan. Use the flat side of the bowl scraper to even out the surface of the marshmallow. Dust the top with 1/4 of the powdered sugar-cornstarch mixture. Cover with plastic wrap and let rest at least 4 hours before cutting.

Dust a chef's knife with some of the remaining powdered sugar-cornstarch mixture. Line a flat surface lined with parchment paper dusted with powdered sugar-cornstarch mixture. Turn marshmallow onto parchment and cut into 1 1/2-inch squares. Dust all sides of cut marshmallows with powdered sugar-cornstarch mixture. Store in an airtight container for up to 2 weeks.

Variations
Hibiscus: Omit vanilla bean. Substitute 3/4 cup water from water-gelatin mixture with 3/4 cup hibiscus tea. To make tea, steep 1/2 cup (25g) dried hibiscus in 3/4 cup boiling water. Cool. Strain and discard hibiscus.
Mango: Omit vanilla bean. Substitute 3/4 cup water from water-gelatin mixture with 1/2 cup mango purée and 1/4 cup orange juice.
Lavender: Omit vanilla bean. Substitute 3/4 cup water from water-gelatin mixture with 3/4 cup lavender tea. To make the tea, steep 1/2 cup fresh lavender in 3/4 cup boiling water for 10 minutes. Strain and discard lavender. Place 1 tablespoon dried lavender buds in spice grinder to coarsely grind. Combine with 1/2 cup sugar to make lavender sugar. Dust nonstick spray-coated baking dish with lavender sugar, pour in lavender marshmallow mixture, and cover with remaining lavender sugar.

CHOCOLATE BARK

A fantastic gift or Friday-night treat. Top with your favorite goodies from your pantry; we have several suggestions below, but the sky's the limit!
Gluten-free, depending on the topping

2 cups (340g) chopped dark chocolate, 70% cacao
Toppings of your choice

Line sheet pan with parchment paper and set aside.

Fill a medium saucepan halfway with water. Bring to a boil and reduce to a simmer. Place chocolate in a clean, dry mixing bowl and nestle on top of saucepan. Use a rubber spatula to gently stir until just melted. Be sure to not add air in while stirring. Remove bowl from saucepan and continue to stir until chocolate is completed melted. Immediately pour onto parchment-lined sheet pan. Sprinkle topping of your choice evenly over chocolate. Refrigerate until set, about 30 minutes. Break into pieces and store in airtight container in a cool, dry place for up to 2 weeks.

Topping Variations
Peppermint: 12 (70g) starlight peppermints, crushed
Friday Night Pretzel Peanut: 3/4 cup (40g) crushed pretzels, 1/4 cup (40g) chopped roasted and salted peanuts, and 1/4 teaspoon Maldon sea salt
Pistachio Cranberry: 1/4 cup (36g) chopped dried cranberries and 1 tablespoon (8g) chopped Sicilian pistachios

GRANOLA

My mom made granola for us kids growing up in New Jersey in the 1960s. All we wanted was Cap'n Crunch.
Thanks, Mom, for always being on the cutting edge—and for taking us to Woodstock.
Gluten-free

Serves 12

1 tablespoon vanilla extract
½ cup (100g) grapeseed oil
½ cup (106g) golden brown sugar, packed
½ cup (156g) maple syrup
4 cups (396g) old-fashioned rolled oats
1 cup (86g) sliced almonds
1 cup (113g) pecan pieces
1 cup (120g) pepitas
1 cup (85g) sweetened shredded coconut
1 cup (114g) dried cranberries
1 cup (150g) dried pears, chopped
1 cup (128g) dried apricots, chopped

Preheat oven to 325°. Combine vanilla extract, grapeseed oil, brown sugar, and maple syrup in a large saucepan over medium heat. Simmer until sugar dissolves. Remove from heat and set aside. Combine oats, almonds, pecan pieces, pepitas, and shredded coconut in a large mixing bowl.

Pour hot sugar liquid over dry ingredients. Stir with a rubber spatula to coat dry ingredients. Lightly coat a parchment-lined sheet pan with nonstick spray. Spread granola evenly onto pan.

Bake, rotating halfway through, until golden brown, about 24 minutes. Allow granola to cool and transfer to a large bowl. Add dried fruit and stir to combine. Store in an aroma-free airtight container for up to 2 weeks.

RAW GRANOLA BARS

We sell a lot of these at the café. They're a great grab-and-go snack.
Gluten-free

Makes 8

1 3/4 cups (174g) old-fashioned rolled oats, toasted

1/2 cup (43g) sliced almonds, toasted

1/2 cup (58g) pecan pieces

3 tablespoons pepitas

1/4 cup (38g) golden raisins

1/4 cup (20g) sweetened shredded coconut

3 tablespoons flaxseeds

1 tablespoon chia seeds

1/2 cup (135g) natural salted creamy almond butter

1/2 cup (172g) brown rice syrup

Lightly coat an 8-inch-square baking pan with nonstick spay.

Mix oats, almonds, pecans, pepitas, raisins, coconut, flaxseeds, and chia seeds together in a large bowl. Set aside.

Combine almond butter and brown rice syrup in a small saucepan over medium heat. Stir with a heat-resistant rubber spatula until combined and almond butter has liquefied. Do not boil or simmer.

Pour wet almond butter mixture over dry ingredients and stir with rubber spatula to coat dry ingredients well. Be careful—the wet mixture may be very hot.

Pour into square pan. Lightly coat an 8-inch-square piece of parchment paper with nonstick spray and place over granola bar mixture. Use a flat-bottomed measuring cup to press down on mixture with even pressure. Knock out any air pockets or gaps. Granola bar will be 3/4 inch thick. Leave to set until cool, at least 2 hours.

When it's cool, remove from the pan and use a chef's knife to cut into 8 pieces, each measuring 2" x 4". Serve immediately or store in an airtight container; they'll keep for up to 2 weeks.

MERINGUE PAVLOVA

Meringue is popular these days, with the need for gluten-free desserts. Dress this up for any occasion. It's a real beauty!
Gluten-free

Makes one 10-inch cake

Meringue

1½ cups (300g) granulated sugar
4 extra-large (¾ cup, or 150g) egg whites, room temperature
1 teaspoon vanilla extract
¼ teaspoon sea salt

Preheat oven to 350°. Spread sugar evenly onto parchment-lined sheet pan. Heat sugar in oven until golden, about 5 minutes.

While sugar is in oven, place egg whites in a clean, dry mixing bowl of a stand mixer fitted with the whisk attachment. Whip egg whites on medium speed until frothy. Carefully lift corners of each side of parchment paper together and pour hot sugar into egg whites. Add vanilla extract and salt. Increase speed to high, and continue to whip until meringue is medium-stiff and glossy.

Lower oven temperature to 200°. Line 2 sheet pans with parchment paper and set aside.

Transfer 3 cups meringue onto one of the sheet pans. Use a rubber spatula or small offset spatula to spread meringue into a 10-inch round shape. Transfer 2 cups meringue onto one half of the second sheet pan. Spread meringue into a 6-inch round. Place remaining 1 cup meringue onto other half of sheet pan. Shape it into a gigantic dollop. Bake until exterior and bottom are dry and firm, about 2 hours. Turn off oven and leave meringue in oven overnight.

Berry Compote

1 cup (150g) fresh or frozen berries,
   such as raspberries, blackberries, and/
   or strawberries, sliced
1/2 cup (100g) granulated sugar

Place berries and sugar in a small
saucepan and cook over medium heat.
Smash the berries and simmer compote
until juices and sugar thicken into a
syrup. Remove from heat and store in a
container in the refrigerator until ready to
use, up to 1 week.

Pastry Cream

1 cup (235g) whole milk
1/4 cup (50g) granulated sugar
1/2 vanilla bean, split lengthwise and
   scraped
1 large egg
1 1/2 tablespoons cornstarch
1/8 teaspoon sea salt
2 tablespoons (28g) unsalted butter

Place milk, sugar, and vanilla bean in a
large stainless steel saucepan and bring
to a scald.

   Whisk egg, cornstarch, and salt
together in a mixing bowl. Whisk
in 1/4 cup warm milk mixture. Continue
to whisk in warm milk in 2 additions.
(Adding the milk all at once will increase
the temperature too rapidly.)

   Return mixture to saucepan and
continuously whisk over medium heat
until it thickens to custard consistency, at
least 15 minutes. Remove from heat and
whisk in butter. Pour into food processor
and blend until smooth. Strain custard
through a chinois or sieve into a medium
mixing bowl. Immediately cover surface
with plastic film to prevent skin from
forming. Place bowl in an ice water bath
to stop cooking. When cool, transfer into
airtight container and refrigerate for up
to 1 week.

Assembly

Meringue
Pastry Cream
3 cups (720g) whipping cream,
   whipped to medium-soft peaks
5 cups fresh berries, such as
   raspberries, blackberries, and/or
   strawberries, sliced
Berry Compote

Place 10-inch meringue round onto
serving platter. Gently spread 1/2 cup
pastry cream onto meringue. Dollop
with 1 1/2 cups whipped cream and
spread 3 cups berries evenly on top.
Drizzle 1/2 cup berry compote on top.
Stack 6-inch meringue round on top.
Gently spread 1 1/2 cups pastry cream
and 1 1/2 cups whipped cream onto
meringue. Top with 1 1/2 cups berries.
Drizzle 1/2 cup berry compote on top.
Stack giant meringue dollop on top.
Decorate with remaining berries. Serve
immediately.

ETON MESS

In this traditional English dessert, the fruit balances the sweetness of the meringue and creates a chewy deliciousness.
Gluten-free

Serves 6

1 1/4 cups (250g) granulated sugar, divided
2 extra-large (1/4 cup + 2 tablespoons or 75g) egg whites, room temperature
1 1/2 teaspoons vanilla extract, divided
1/4 teaspoon sea salt
4 cups (600g) fresh strawberries, sliced
1 teaspoon vanilla extract
4 cups (960g) heavy whipping cream, whipped to medium-soft peaks

Preheat oven to 350°. Spread 3/4 cup (150g) sugar evenly onto parchment-lined sheet pan. Heat sugar in oven until golden, about 5 minutes.

While sugar is in oven, place egg whites in a clean, dry mixing bowl of a stand mixer fitted with the whisk attachment. Whip egg whites on medium speed until frothy. Carefully lift corners of each side of parchment paper together and pour hot sugar into egg whites. Add 1/2 teaspoon vanilla extract and salt. Increase speed to high and continue to whip until meringue is medium-stiff and glossy.

Lower oven temperature to 200°. Line sheet pan with parchment paper. Dollop 12 even portions of meringue onto parchment-lined sheet pan. Space the meringues 1/2 inch apart. Bake until exterior and bottom are dry and firm, about 2 hours. Turn off oven and leave in oven overnight. Store in airtight container for up to 1 week.

Toss sliced strawberries with 1/2 cup (100g) sugar and 1 teaspoon vanilla extract. Set aside to allow strawberries to macerate for 15 minutes.

Break meringues into large chunks and place into serving cups or bowls. Top with 1/2 cup whipped cream and 1/2 cup strawberries. Continue to assemble with large chunks of meringue, cream, and strawberries. Serve immediately.

COCONUT CHIA PUDDING WITH SEEDED STREUSEL

I find it funny that the seed paste we spread on our chia pets in the '70s is now going into our kids' pudding. Cha-cha-cha chia! The seeds are a good source of fiber and antioxidants. Serve with whatever fruit is most delicious at that moment.

Gluten-free

Serves 6

Coconut Chia Pudding

¼ cup (40g) chia seeds
1 cup (222g) boiling water
1½ cups (360g) coconut milk

Place chia seeds in a small mixing bowl. Add boiling water and mix well.

Set aside for 5 minutes, allowing chia seeds to absorb all the water. The chia seeds will plump up and become gelatinous. Stir in coconut milk. Transfer pudding to a covered container and chill in refrigerator overnight.

Seeded Streusel

2 tablespoons golden brown sugar, packed
3 tablespoons granulated sugar
½ cup (76g) brown rice flour
¼ cup (35g) sunflower seeds
¼ cup (22g) sliced almonds
¼ cup (25g) old-fashioned rolled oats
¼ cup (34g) flaxseeds
¼ cup (57g) unsalted butter, cut into ½-inch pieces and chilled
⅛ teaspoon sea salt

In the bowl of a stand mixer fitted with the paddle attachment, combine sugars, rice flour, sunflower seeds, almonds, oats, and flaxseeds on low speed. Add butter and salt. Continue to mix on low speed until mixture resembles wet sand, about 5 minutes. Check consistency by grabbing a handful of streusel: it should hold its shape for a few seconds and then crumble.

Preheat oven to 375°. Spread streusel evenly onto a parchment-lined sheet pan. Bake for 10 minutes. The edges will crisp up first, so use a large offset spatula to stir the streusel, moving the center to the edges to ensure even baking. Bake until golden brown, about 10 more minutes. Cool and transfer to an airtight container.

Assembly

Coconut Pudding
Seeded Streusel
Seasonal fruit

Spoon ½ cup pudding into each bowl. Top with ⅓ cup streusel and garnish with seasonal fruit. Serve.

PANNA COTTA

Italian for cooked cream, panna cotta is an easy dessert that's requested by all our customers. Add your favorite seasonal fruit—I love fuyu persimmons! (Pomegranate seeds are pictured here... also delicious.) *Gluten-free*

Serves 6

1 tablespoon cold water
1 1/2 tablespoons (12g) powdered gelatin
1 cup (200g) granulated sugar
1 vanilla bean, split lengthwise and scraped
2 1/4 cups (540g) heavy whipping cream
3 cups + 2 tablespoons (700g) buttermilk
1 teaspoon lemon juice
1/8 teaspoon sea salt

Place cold water in small mixing bowl. Whisk water and gelatin together and allow gelatin to bloom (absorb the liquid), about 5 minutes.

Place sugar, vanilla bean, and vanilla bean seeds in a medium saucepan. Rub the vanilla bean with sugar to release all the seeds. Add cream and bring to a simmer, stirring occasionally with a rubber spatula to dissolve sugar. Remove from heat. Add bloomed gelatin to cream mixture. Strain into a medium mixing bowl.

Whisk in buttermilk, lemon juice, and salt. Pour into 8-ounce serving bowls or cups. Chill overnight in the refrigerator (uncovered, to prevent condensation from building and falling back into the custard). Garnish with seasonal fresh fruit, if you like, and serve.

BROWN BUTTER ICE CREAM

No ice cream machine needed for this recipe!
Gluten-free

Makes 1 quart

3/4 cup (171g) unsalted butter
1 cup (240g) heavy whipping cream
8 egg yolks, room temperature
3/4 cup + 2 tablespoons (175g) granulated sugar, divided
1 1/4 teaspoons sea salt
4 egg whites, room temperature

Place butter in small saucepan and bring to a boil. After first foam, stir with rubber spatula and scrape bottom of pan to prevent milk solids from burning. Let foam a second time; butter will brown and smell nutty. Remove from heat and set aside.

In the bowl of a stand mixer fitted with the whisk attachment, whisk cream on medium high speed until medium peaks form, about 5 minutes. Transfer to a medium bowl. Cover and chill in refrigerator.

In the clean, dry bowl of a stand mixer fitted with the whisk attachment, whisk egg yolks on medium-high speed. Slowly pour in 1/2 cup (100g) sugar and whisk until thick ribbons form, about 3 minutes. Decrease speed to low and stream in browned butter. Scrape saucepan well, adding all the brown bits. Whisk on medium speed for 2 minutes. Transfer yolk mixture into a large bowl.

In the clean, dry bowl of a stand mixer fitted with the whisk attachment, whisk egg whites on medium-high speed until frothy, about 1 minute. Decrease speed to medium and slowly add remaining sugar. Continue to whisk on medium-high until meringue is medium-stiff.

Remove whipped cream from refrigerator. Use a balloon whisk to gently fold whipped cream into yolk mixture. Mixture should be streaky. Fold in meringue. Make sure to not knock out air. (The balloon whisk will maintain the aeration of the meringue better than a regular piano whisk.) Drag balloon whisk through center of mixture and up against the side of the bowl and allow meringue to fall back into the ice cream mixture to incorporate. Turn the bowl 1/4 clockwise and continue to fold meringue in this manner until it is incorporated, with a few streaks remaining. Mixture should feel light and airy.

Pour into a 1-quart container and place a piece of plastic film directly on top of mixture to prevent any ice crystals from forming. Wrap container well with more plastic film and freeze overnight. May be frozen for up to 1 week.

GOLDEN MILK LATTE

Cecilia and I are crazy for turmeric. We use it as much as possible, and we love it in this drink, which is delicious hot or cold.

Note: You'll need a centrifugal extraction mixer to make the turmeric and ginger juices, unless you have a place to buy the juices ready to go.
Gluten-free

Makes 4 6-ounce servings

½ cup (170g) turmeric juice (made from about 12 ounces to 1 pound turmeric root)
¼ cup (85g) ginger juice (made from 5 to 8 ounces ginger root)
2 tablespoons wildflower honey
1 cup (225g) almond milk
½ cup (120g) coconut milk

In a medium bowl, whisk together turmeric juice, ginger juice, and honey until well blended. Use immediately or store in a container in the refrigerator for up to 3 days. Fine pulp from turmeric and ginger roots will settle, so give it a good whisk before using.

Place almond milk and coconut milk in a medium saucepan and bring to a simmer. Remove from heat and whisk in turmeric–ginger juice mixture. Serve hot or over ice.

HOT CHOCOLATE

A little added cream makes this cocoa extra delicious.
Gluten-free

Serves 8

1/4 cup (50g) granulated sugar
2 3/4 cups (468g) chopped dark chocolate, 70% cacao
2 cups (480g) heavy whipping cream
4 1/2 cups (1058g) whole milk

Place sugar, chocolate, and cream in a large saucepan over medium heat. Whisk constantly to prevent chocolate from burning. Add milk 1 cup at a time. Continue to whisk mixture until chocolate melts completely and mixture simmers. Remove from heat and serve immediately.

MEXICAN HOT CHOCOLATE

The heat from the cayenne and the spice from the cinnamon make this hot chocolate a house favorite.
Gluten-free

Serves 8

2 cinnamon sticks, toasted
1/4 cup (50g) granulated sugar
2 3/4 cups (468g) chopped dark chocolate, 70% cacao
2 cups (480g) heavy whipping cream
1/2 teaspoon ground cayenne pepper
1/2 teaspoon ground cinnamon
4 1/2 cups (1058g) whole milk

Place cinnamon sticks, sugar, chocolate, and cream in a large saucepan over medium heat. Whisk constantly to prevent chocolate from burning. Add cayenne and ground cinnamon and continue to whisk. Add whole milk 1 cup at a time. Continue to whisk until chocolate melts completely and mixture simmers. Remove from heat and strain. Discard cinnamon sticks. Serve immediately.

GLUTEN-FREE RECIPES

VEGAN RECIPES

THANK YOU

The Little Flower Staff

Gustavo Aguilera
Alyson Bourne
Miguel Camacho
Anthony Correa
Lisa Ellison
Jillian Forney
Angie Galvan
Jesus Galvan
Maria Galvan
Stephany Heras
Manuel Jasso
Ashley Johnson
Denise Karr
Shelley Kimura
Cecilia Leung
Noe Martinez
Stephanie Matus
Andy Moreno
Kimberly Murray
Moises Perez
Hermonio Perez DeLeon
Samuel Price
Cecilia Sanchez
Deisy Tostado
Gabriel Vega

Also

Colleen Bates
Fran Berger
Mike & Stephanie Bollenbacher
Sascha Bos
Susan Cohen
Mary Coquillard
Andrea Dombrowski
Jen Ferro
Jonathan Gold
Clemence Gossett
Dan Hare
Amy Inouye
Pat Jalbert-Levine
Roxana Jullapat
Beth Katz, Mt. Washington Pottery
Jeanne Kelley
Evan Kleiman
Joan McNamara
Amanda Millet
Ramsey Naito
Chuck Novak
Patti Peck
Mike Rhodes
Jenna Turner
Staci Valentine
Robert Wemischner

INDEX

Published by Prospect Park Books
2359 Lincoln Avenue
Altadena, California 91001
www.prospectparkbooks.com

Distributed by Consortium Books Sales & Distribution
www.cbsd.com

Library of Congress Cataloging in Publication Data is on file with the Library of Congress. The following is for reference only:

Moore, Christine
Little Flower Baking / by Christine Moore – 1st ed.
     p. cm.
ISBN: 978-1-938849-60-2
1. Dessert and baking. 2. Cooking, American. 3. Cooking, French. I. Title.

Recipe development & testing by Cecilia Leung
Edited by Colleen Dunn Bates
Editorial assistant Sascha Bos
Proofreader Pat Jalbert-Levine

Photography by Staci Valentine
Photo styling by Jeanne Kelley
Designed by Amy Inouye, Future Studio

First edition

Printed in China by Imago on sustainably produced paper

ABOUT THE TEAM

The Kitchen Crew

Author Christine Moore is the owner of the Little Flower Candy Co. and the chef/owner of Little Flower Cafe and Lincoln restaurant, both in Pasadena, California. A pastry chef who trained in Paris and Los Angeles, Moore is the author of *Little Flower: Recipes from the Cafe*, which has earned praise from everyone from David Lebovitz to the *Wall Street Journal*. She sells her candy nationwide and has developed a passionate following for her exceptionally flavorful baked goods and café food at both restaurants.

Contributing author Cecilia Leung has been Little Flower's pastry chef since 2010, after baking at such leading Los Angeles restaurants as Spago, Grace, and JiRaffe.

The Photo Crew

Los Angeles-based photographer Staci Valentine has also photographed such books as *The Seasonal Jewish Kitchen, Das Cookbook, Tomatomania,* and *Masumoto: Perfect Peach*. Photo stylist Jeanne Kelley is the author of several cookbooks, including *The Portable Feast, Kitchen Garden, Salad for Dinner,* and *Blue Eggs and Yellow Tomatoes*.

Left to right: Staci Valentine, Christine Moore, Cecilia Leung, Jeanne Kelley